JUST AS I
HAM

JUST AS I
HAM

OVER 100 HEAVENLY RECIPES
FOR COVERED DISH COOKING

JANE AND MARK
JARRELL

BROADMAN
& HOLMAN
PUBLISHERS

Nashville, Tennessee

0-8054-0176-8

Published by Broadman & Holman Publishers, Nashville, Tennessee
Page Design: Anderson Thomas Design
Page Composition: PerfecType, Nashville, Tennessee
Editor: Vicki Crumpton
Illustrations: Bill Ross

Dewey Decimal Classification: 641.5
Subject Heading: COOKING/ENTERTAINING/QUANTITY COOKING
Library of Congress Card Catalog Number: 98-16055

All Scripture citation is from the Holy Bible, King James Version.

Library of Congress Cataloging-in-Publication Data
Jarrell, Jane Cabaniss, 1961–
    Just as I ham : Over 100 heavenly recipes for covered dish cooking/Jane and
    Mark Jarrell.
        p. cm.
    ISBN 0-8054-0176-8 (pbk.)
    1. Cookery. 2. Entertaining. 3. Quantity cookery. I. Jarrell, Mark, 1958–. II. Title.
TX714.J37   1997
641.5'7—dc21
                                                                        98-16055
                                                                        CIP

1 2 3 4 5 02 01 00 99 98

IN DEDICATION

To our Grandmothers, only one of whom remains with us. In their homes and kitchens, we first experienced the joy of generations of family gathering around the dining room table. With the love and laughter that only a grandmother can give, our most precious memories were made.

OPLE RICHARDSON COLLARD

GRACE PEAVY JARRELL

ANNIE JETER HULL

GERTRUDE BEAM CABANISS

CONTENTS

ACKNOWLEDGMENTS

Many thanks to all of the friends and family who helped us locate church cookbooks from across the country. Your help and support is much appreciated.

INTRODUCTION

S ome of our fondest memories are of the times we spend sitting around the table. Passing the black-eyed peas or cutting that second piece of pound cake helps us realize that cookery is a means of communication. Recipes shared from generation to generation give us a glimpse into the world of yesteryear, joining the past with the present. Great foods are a legacy. After all, who in their right mind would hand down a bad recipe?

Whether a humble family meal, grand entertaining with the fine china, or a special holiday extravaganza, the food we share unites us. It is the heavenly hospitality and fellowship we remember, but the food is what brings us together. Have you ever been to a social occasion worth its salt where food did not play a major role? So what is it about food that draws people together?

Of course we come to eat—to taste—but food satisfies other senses. First, you eat with your eyes; what looks good to you will often motivate you to pick up that huge, stainless steel spoon and plop a serving on your Chinet plate. What smells good to you will do the same. The crunch of a warm piece of fried chicken and the creamy texture of a cooked custard also play a role in your eating satisfaction. This sharing of food, this celebration of the senses, is a part of what this book is about, plus some added funnies that are sure to remind you of someone you know. You will find an added dimension; these recipes were culled out of church cookbooks from across the country for the best of the best, the crème de la crème, of covered dish recipes. Friends, families, and churches submitted their best and most unique recipes to share with others. The recipes were selected and tested to give you some new choices for your next important memory-making get-together.

We have also stirred in some how-tos for when you are feeding the flock. Just how many loaves and fishes are needed when the guest list is huge? What if you are taking your party on the road? We have you covered with a section on the remote covered dish and the must-haves for that special event.

Through good times and heartache, organizations, churches, and family reunions have not forgotten the power of a great covered dish. Just choose the time of day, and you can produce a perfect menu from this book in less time than it takes the butter to soften. Food, fun, and fellowship is the key—so go ahead, call a few friends and ask them to get out their Corningware, stainless steel slotted spoons, and lawn chairs. It's time for a covered dish experience.

DOBBER'S
DEAD

ho could forget the famous scene in the musical *Oklahoma!* in which Curly and Jed were bidding on the boxed supper prepared by sweet Laurey, (later known as Mrs. Partridge), and the hero lost the bid? Poor Laurey had to endure unwanted advances by the repulsive and badly-in-need-of-a-shave Jed, all in the name of raising money for a good cause. Well, that's mild in comparison to what poor Dobber McIlhenny suffered at the hands of his wife Doris at our last fund-raiser for the beautification of the Piggly Wiggly parking lot.

Dobber never was real sharp. You might say the elevator didn't reach the top floor; but bless his heart he tried hard to please Doris though she rarely appreciated the efforts. Doris was known far and wide for her fluffy biscuits and her prize-winning watermelon rind preserves. Her nemesis, Jewel Jernigan, had also won blue ribbons for her strawberry-rhubarb preserves, much to Doris's dismay. It didn't take a rocket scientist to figure out that the last basket Doris wanted Dobber to bid on for a supper would be Jewel's. But, like I said earlier, Dobber's lights were on, but no one was home.

The bidding had just begun when Doris nudged Dobber and told him, "I'll let you know when I want you to start bidding."

A few minutes later, Jewel's brightly decorated basket, with faux gems hot-glued all over the handle, came up for bid. Doris let out a loud "Humph" to show her contempt. Dim-witted Dobber mistook that sound as his cue to start the bidding.

"Forty-five dollars!" he hollered out as Doris sat momentarily dumbstruck by what was happening. The auctioneer took the bid and asked for fifty.

"Fifty dollars," said one of Jewel's cousins, who owed her several favors.

"Seventy-five dollars!" sang out Dobber. Doris had come back to her senses by now and rewarded Dobber with a sound thump on the head with the flyswatter she always kept handy for occasions such as these.

That'll shut the old fool up, she thought to herself. *What has gotten into him, trying to buy that piece of trash?* she wondered.

Dobber's bald head had a red imprint of the flyswatter net, and he was a little dazed by the force of the blow. Thinking that his wife meant to spur him on, he renewed his efforts to win the bidding.

"One hundred dollars!" There was dead silence for a moment. No one in the history of our town had ever received a bid of one hundred dollars for a boxed supper. Jewel swelled up with pride. Doris was so angry she couldn't see straight, and Dobber was grinning from ear to ear, convinced that he had done a great thing for his wife.

"Sold for one hundred dollars!!" sang out the auctioneer as he held out the bejeweled basket to Dobber. As Dobber got up and started to make his way to the front, Doris just lost it. She started yelling and stomping her feet.

She was having a real conniption fit until she blew a gasket and just passed out cold. Dobber rushed back to her side with the basket and attempted to revive her with a swig of Jewel's lime sherbet punch from the thermos. As she sputtered and coughed back to life, you could see in her eyes that Dobber's days on this earth were numbered.

APPETIZERS

 = *"A piece of cake"* (quick and easy)

ARMADILLO EGGS   *Makes 10 servings*

1 JAR WHOLE JALAPEÑO PEPPERS
1 ½ CUPS CHEDDAR CHEESE, GRATED
1 POUND BULK HOT SAUSAGE
10 CANNED BISCUITS, UNCOOKED

Preheat oven to 450°.

1. Remove and discard the pepper stems. Slit peppers lengthwise, rinse, and stuff with cheese. (Caution: Be careful in handling peppers; use gloves or wash hands carefully before touching eyes, face, etc.)

2. Pat sausage into thin patties, and wrap patties around the stuffed peppers, placing the seamed side down in a baking dish.

3. Bake until the sausage is cooked. Drain grease and set sausage and peppers aside.

4. Roll out each biscuit. Place a sausage-wrapped pepper at one end and roll up. Place on baking sheet. Bake at 450° until the biscuits are browned.

DENISE TIGERT
Heritage Presbyterian Church
Oklahoma City, Oklahoma

ALOHA DIP   *Makes 2 ½ cups*

1 (8 OUNCE) PACKAGE CREAM CHEESE, SOFTENED TO ROOM TEMPERATURE
3 TABLESPOONS APPLE JUICE
1 CUP SHREDDED COCONUT
1 CUP CHOPPED NUTS
1 (6 OUNCE) CAN CRUSHED PINEAPPLE

1. Blend all ingredients together. Chill.

2. Serve with gingersnaps, fruits, or use as a topping for gelatin desserts.

CARROLL STEWART
First United Methodist Church
Edmond, Oklahoma

COBY'S
ARTICHOKE BALLS *Makes 1 dozen*

1 (8 OUNCE) CAN ARTICHOKE HEARTS
2 CLOVES GARLIC, FINELY CHOPPED
2 TABLESPOONS OLIVE OIL
2 EGGS, LIGHTLY BEATEN
½ CUP ROMANO CHEESE, GRATED OR CRUMBLED
½ CUP ITALIAN BREAD CRUMBS

Preheat oven to 350°.

1. Place artichoke hearts in a medium-size bowl and mash.

2. Sauté garlic in olive oil.

3. Add artichokes and eggs.

4. Cook 5 minutes, stirring to mix well.

5. Blend in cheese and bread crumbs. Form into small balls.

6. Place balls on a cookie sheet and bake for 6 to 8 minutes.

BETTY JEAN PEARCE
Forest Hills United Methodist Church
Brentwood, Tennessee

APPETIZER PARTY CRACKERS *Makes 4 cups*

2 (10 OUNCE) PACKAGES OYSTER CRACKERS
1 (1 OUNCE) PACKAGE DRY RANCH SALAD DRESSING
  MIX
1 1/2 TEASPOONS DILL WEED
1/2 TEASPOON GARLIC POWDER
1/2 TEASPOON LEMON PEPPER
1 CUP VEGETABLE OIL

1. Empty crackers into a large bowl.

2. Pour all remaining ingredients into a small bowl. Mix well.

3. Pour mixture over crackers and stir.

4. Allow to sit for about 2 hours. Stir frequently with a rubber spatula.

5. Cover and store in an airtight container.

JACQUIE LEE
Taste and See
Great Hills Baptist Church
Austin, Texas

ZUCCHINI FRITTATA *Makes 12 servings*

3 CUPS THINLY SLICED ZUCCHINI
1/3 CUP RED ONION, DICED
1/4 CUP FRESH PARSLEY, CHOPPED
1 CLOVE GARLIC, MINCED
1 CUP BISCUIT MIX
1/2 CUP VEGETABLE OIL
1/2 TEASPOON SALT
1/4 TEASPOON BASIL
1/4 TEASPOON OREGANO
1/4 TEASPOON BLACK PEPPER
1/2 CUP PARMESAN CHEESE, GRATED
4 EGGS

Preheat oven to 350°.

1. Combine all ingredients in a large bowl. Mix well.

2. Pour into a greased 9- x 11-inch baking pan.

3. Bake for 25 minutes or until golden brown.

BARBARA LACY
Grizzly Flats: Favorite Recipes from Our Best Cooks
Grizzly Flats, California

SUE DUNN'S CHEESE APPLE BALL *Makes 2 1/2 cups*

1 POUND HOOP CHEESE, GRATED
2 (8 OUNCE) PACKAGES CREAM CHEESE, SOFTENED
   TO ROOM TEMPERATURE
2 (5 OUNCE) JARS KRAFT PIMIENTO CHEESE SPREAD
1 SMALL ONION, FINELY GRATED
¾ TEASPOON CAYENNE PEPPER
3 TABLESPOONS DURKEE SALAD DRESSING
1 CLOVE GARLIC, PRESSED
2 TABLESPOONS LEA & PERRINS SAUCE
1 TABLESPOON PREPARED MUSTARD
PAPRIKA

1. Cream cheeses at low speed in mixer until fluffy. Blend in remaining ingredients, except paprika.

2. Cover and chill until firm (about 3 or 4 hours).

3. Mold into desired shape (in this case, an apple).

4. Sprinkle with paprika.

5. Serve with favorite crackers or vegetables.

SUE SMITH
In memory of Sue Dunn
First Baptist Church
Pine Bluff, Arkansas

CHICKEN BITES *Makes 6 dozen*

4 CHICKEN BREASTS, BONED, SPLIT, AND SKINNED
1 CUP ROUND BUTTERY CRACKERS, FINELY CRUSHED
$\frac{1}{2}$ CUP PARMESAN CHEESE, GRATED
$\frac{1}{4}$ CUP WALNUTS, FINELY CHOPPED
$\frac{1}{2}$ TEASPOON SEASONED SALT
1 TEASPOON DRIED THYME
1 TEASPOON DRIED BASIL LEAVES
$\frac{1}{4}$ TEASPOON BLACK PEPPER
$\frac{1}{2}$ CUP (1 STICK) BUTTER OR MARGARINE, MELTED

Preheat oven to 400°.

1. Cover baking sheets with aluminum foil.

2. Cut chicken into 1-inch pieces.

3. Mix cracker crumbs, cheese, walnuts, seasoned salt, thyme, basil, and pepper.

4. Dip chicken into the melted butter, then roll in the crumb mixture.

5. Place chicken pieces about ½-inch apart on prepared baking sheets.

6. Bake, uncovered, until golden brown, about 20 to 25 minutes.

JEAN LAPRADE GRAHAM
The Jubilee of Our Many Blessings Cookbook
Highland Park United Methodist Church
Dallas, Texas

CRAB DIP *Makes 2 ½ cups*

1 (8 OUNCE) PACKAGE CREAM CHEESE, SOFTENED TO
   ROOM TEMPERATURE
1 MEDIUM ONION, FINELY CHOPPED
1 (12 OUNCE) BOTTLE COCKTAIL SAUCE
1 (6½ OUNCE) CAN CRABMEAT
PARSLEY FLAKES

1. Spread cream cheese evenly over the bottom of a shallow dish.

2. Sprinkle chopped onion on top of the cream cheese.

3. Pour cocktail sauce over onions (just enough to cover; do not spread cocktail sauce too thick).

4. Sprinkle crabmeat over cocktail sauce. Top with parsley flakes.

5. Serve with favorite crackers.

RICHARD KYLE THUNE
Rose of Sharon Family Cookbook
Rose of Sharon Lutheran Church
Cottage Grove, Minnesota

HOLIDAY SQUARES FLORENTINO *Makes 40 servings*

4 EGGS, BEATEN
1 (10¾ OUNCE) CAN CREAM OF MUSHROOM SOUP
2 (10 OUNCE) PACKAGES FROZEN CHOPPED SPINACH,
   THAWED, WELL DRAINED, AND MINCED
¼ CUP GREEN ONIONS, MINCED
½ CUP WALNUTS, TOASTED AND CHOPPED
1 CUP SWISS CHEESE, SHREDDED
¼ CUP PARMESAN CHEESE, GRATED
1 (8 OUNCE) PACKAGE REFRIGERATED CRESCENT
   ROLLS

Preheat oven to 350°.

1. In a large bowl, combine all ingredients except rolls. Mix well.

2. Unroll crescent rolls, but do not separate. Press into bottom of a 9- x 13-inch buttered baking pan; press seams together.

3. Spread spinach mixture over dough.

4. Bake for 40 minutes or until knife inserted in center comes out clean.

5. Cut into 1-inch pieces.

MITZI DAVIS
Church on the Rock Family Cookbook
Church on the Rock
Dallas, Texas

SWEET RED PEPPER AND ALMOND DIP   *Makes about 3 cups*

1 (1 OUNCE) POUCH DRY ONION SOUP MIX
1 CUP SOUR CREAM
1 CUP PLAIN YOGURT
1/3 CUP SWEET RED BELL PEPPER, CHOPPED
1/3 CUP ALMONDS, TOASTED AND CHOPPED

1. In a medium bowl, combine all ingredients. Mix well.

2. Cover and refrigerate at least 2 hours before serving.

3. Serve with crackers, chips, or vegetables.

CAROL MARTIN
Inspiring Recipes
First Baptist Church
Macedon, New York

PEPPER NUTS   *Makes 4 dozen*

3 STICKS BUTTER (NOT MARGARINE), SOFTENED TO
   ROOM TEMPERATURE
1 1/2 CUPS SUGAR
2 EGGS
5 CUPS ALL-PURPOSE FLOUR
1 TEASPOON BLACK PEPPER
1 TEASPOON BAKING POWDER

Preheat oven to 350°.

1. Cream butter and sugar until well blended. Add eggs one at a time, beating well after each addition.

2. Mix the dry ingredients and add to the creamed mixture. Mix well.

3. Form into long, finger-size rolls and wrap in wax paper. Chill for several hours.

4. Slice into ½-inch slices and place on baking sheet.

5. Bake for 7 to 10 minutes until light brown.

CHARLOTTE HISLOP
Sing for Your Supper Again
First Baptist Church
West Monroe, Louisiana

BLUE RIBBON WATERMELON RIND PRESERVES *Makes about 10 pints*

10 POUNDS MELON RIND, PEELED
CRUSHED ICE
10 CUPS WATER
10 POUNDS SUGAR, DIVIDED IN HALF
2 DOZEN WHOLE CLOVES
2 STICKS CINNAMON, BROKEN
1 TEASPOON SALT
4 LEMONS, SLICED
4 ORANGES, SLICED

1. Peel melon rind by removing pink peel as close to hard rind as possible.

2. Cut melon rind in strips and then into small squares.

3. Place in a large container and add crushed ice.

4. Let stand in the refrigerator overnight.

5. Wash thoroughly twice.

6. Place rind in a large pan and add 10 cups water and half the sugar.

7. Tie the spices in a small gauze or cheesecloth bag and add to the rind mixture.

8. Add salt.

9. Place on medium heat on the stove and cook for 4 hours.

10. Add remaining sugar and sliced lemons and oranges; cook until the rinds are clear. (It will get foamy on the top.)

11. Place cooked rinds in pint canning jars and seal according to manufac-turer's directions. (As it cools the syrup will thicken.)

IDA PAPERT
Papert Family Cookbook
Dallas, Texas

THE SWEET
BEYOND

When spring is in the air and the leaves are tender green on the trees, my thoughts turn to the annual pleasant picnic on the grounds. The Pleasant Rest cemetery grounds, that is. Now before you think that I am some sort of weird tombstone-reading, hysterical/historical society member, let me explain.

Where I come from, my church sponsors a covered dish luncheon each year at the Heavenly Slumber Pavilion, followed by a cleaning of the cemetery. Every spring you can count on the same Kentucky Fried Chicken from Mavis Bilwater stuck on her own plate and wrapped in foil like she just pulled it from her own oven, dozens of deviled eggs whipped, piped and paprikaed to death (the pros have their own decorative egg holder dishes) and angel food cakes so high, it's like eating sweet air.

There's always plenty for everyone to eat, but there wouldn't be if every-body fixed as much food as Darlene Dillard. She brings all five of her children and one bowl of lima beans that might feed three people that don't care for limas. But, you know, the good Lord has funny ways of dealing with people who aren't cheerful givers.

Just ask Darlene about what happened to her at our last grave sweeping. Poor woman nearly died of fright! Not only did Darlene tend to be stingy with her cov-ered dish, she was also slack on her cleanup duties for her assigned grave sites. Notice I said "was," because I guarantee you that Darlene is a changed woman.

From the reports I received, Darlene had set out to the newest section of the cemetery, *The Sweet Beyond*, with her broom and trash bags right after lunch on that fine day last year. Apparently, she decided that a nice, peaceful nap would be just the thing with not a living soul around to disturb her. She laid down beside a gravesite and closed her eyes, but the sun was shining right in her face, making it hard to rest. Sitting up, she looked all around for a shady spot, when she spied a long, white cloth lying on the ground, left behind from the last service. It was perfect for blocking those pesky sun rays and actually protected her whole body. Must have felt comfy cozy because Darlene soon drifted off to a deep slumber.

While Darlene got in her forty winks, Pleasant Rest's newest employee, Jackson Mitchell, was digging his first grave not twenty feet away, but hidden by a hedge of thick shrubbery. After he finished digging, Jackson radioed his boss that he was ready for the body to be delivered. The boss said he would send the corpse right over, but he got involved trying to tone down the pur-ple in Mrs. Bottoms' hair and forgot all about the call. Meanwhile, Jackson took a bathroom break nearby and returned by way of Darelene's nap site. *Well, thanks a lot for just dropping the body off without waiting or even trying to help me,* he thought to himself as he went to bring the stretcher back.

You know where this story is heading by now! Would you believe that Darlene did not wake until the first shovel of dirt hit her right smack dab on the forehead. It was hard to say who was scared the worst: Darlene, upon finding herself about to be buried alive, or Jackson, having his corpse sit up and scream, "Help me, Jesus!"

We can all rest easier knowing that Darlene Dillard got the wakeup call of her life. Let's just say that it's highly doubtful that she will be lying down on the job at this year's cleaning! Now if we could just get her to bring more beans. . . .

COME LETTUCE ADORE HIM
SALADS
AND SOUPS

 = *"A piece of cake"* (*quick and easy*)

JANE'S PASTA SALAD   *Makes 6 servings*

1/2 POUND ROTINI, COOKED
1 CUP ITALIAN DRESSING
1/2 CUP PARMESAN CHEESE, GRATED

OPTIONAL AMOUNTS OF ANY OF THE FOLLOWING:
   CHEESE CUBES
   SLICED OLIVES
   ARTICHOKE HEARTS
   HAM CUBES
   TUNA
   BROCCOLI
   GREEN BELL PEPPER
   GREEN ONIONS
   CHOPPED CELERY
   CHOPPED TOMATO
   CHUNKS OF AVOCADO

1. Toss pasta with dressing and grated cheese.

2. Stir in any of the other ingredients, except the tomato and avocado.

3. Chill for several hours.

4. Add tomato and avocado (and maybe more dressing and cheese) before serving.

JANE NEWKIRK
Mira Mesa Presbyterian Church
San Diego, California

TOMATO AND FRESH BASIL PASTA SALAD   *Makes 8 servings*

3 1/2 POUNDS FRESH TOMATOES, PEELED, SEEDED,
   AND CHOPPED
1 TEASPOON HONEY
3 CLOVES GARLIC, MINCED
1/2 CUP EXTRA-VIRGIN OLIVE OIL

2 TABLESPOONS FRESH BASIL, CHOPPED OR
  2 TEASPOONS DRIED
3 TABLESPOONS PARSLEY, CHOPPED
1 SCALLION, CHOPPED
2 TABLESPOONS LEMON JUICE
1 TABLESPOON RED WINE VINEGAR
1/4 TEASPOON SALT
FRESHLY GROUND BLACK PEPPER
1 (16 OUNCE) PACKAGE BOW TIE PASTA, COOKED

1. Sauté tomatoes, honey, and garlic in olive oil until most of the liquid evaporates and the mixture is thickened. Stir frequently to prevent burning.

2. Pour into a bowl and add the remaining ingredients, except pasta. Mix well.

3. After the sauce has cooled, toss with the cooked pasta.

4. Garnish with additional basil leaves and chopped scallions.

JO LOGAN
First United Methodist Church
Edmond, Oklahoma

HAM AND RICE SALAD *Makes 6 servings*

1 1/3 CUPS LONG GRAIN RICE, COOKED
1/4 CUP FRENCH DRESSING
3/4 CUP MAYONNAISE
1 TABLESPOON GREEN ONION, FINELY CHOPPED
1/2 TEASPOON SALT
1/2 TEASPOON CURRY POWDER
1/2 TEASPOON DRY MUSTARD
BLACK PEPPER, TO TASTE
1 1/2 CUPS HAM STRIPS
1 CUP RAW CAULIFLOWER, SLICED
1 (10 OUNCE) PACKAGE FROZEN PEAS, COOKED
1/2 CUP CELERY, THINLY SLICED
1/2 CUP RADISHES, THINLY SLICED

1. Toss rice and French dressing. Chill for several hours or overnight.

2. Combine mayonnaise, onion, salt, curry powder, mustard, and pepper.

3. Add to rice mixture. Stir well to blend.

4. Add remaining ingredients. Mix well.

MRS. ROBERT E. FARRIS
Viands and Vittles
Forest Hills United Methodist Church
Brentwood, Tennessee

 # LAVENDER DELIGHT *Makes 8 servings*

1 (29 OUNCE) CAN OR 3 ½ CUPS PEARS IN SYRUP
1 (3 OUNCE) PACKAGE BLACKBERRY GELATIN
1 (8 OUNCE) PACKAGE CREAM CHEESE, SOFTENED TO
  ROOM TEMPERATURE
1 CUP WHIPPING CREAM

1. Drain pears, reserving 1 cup syrup.

2. Bring syrup to a boil. Dissolve gelatin in syrup. Cool.

3. Put cooled gelatin, cream cheese, and pears into blender. Blend until smooth.

4. Pour into a large bowl and chill in the refrigerator for about 1½ hours, or until quite thick.

5. Whip cream and fold into thickened gelatin mixture. Beat until fluffy and well blended.

6. Pour into a well-oiled, 6-cup ring mold. Chill overnight.

KAY NUDD
Catholic Church of Saint Walter
Roselle, Illinois

ORANGE SHERBET SALAD
Makes 4 servings

1 (6 OUNCE) PACKAGE ORANGE JELL-O
2 CUPS BOILING WATER
1 PINT ORANGE SHERBET
1 (11 OUNCE) CAN MANDARIN ORANGES
1 (6 OUNCE) CAN CRUSHED PINEAPPLE

1. Dissolve gelatin in 2 cups boiling water.

2. Add sherbet and stir until dissolved.

3. Add remaining ingredients. Place in refrigerator until firm.

CINDY SANDERS
Sing for Your Supper Again
First Baptist Church
West Monroe, Louisiana

LAYERED LETTUCE SALAD
Makes 6 to 8 servings

1 HEAD OF ICEBERG LETTUCE, TORN INTO PIECES
10 SLICES CRISP FRIED BACON, CRUMBLED
6 HARD-BOILED EGGS, PEELED AND CHOPPED
1 (10 OUNCE) PACKAGE FROZEN GREEN PEAS (I USE
   ABOUT $1/2$ OF THE PACKAGE)
1 BUNCH GREEN ONIONS, CHOPPED
$1 1/2$ TO 2 CUPS SALAD DRESSING
1 TO 2 TABLESPOONS SUGAR

1. Layer lettuce, bacon, eggs, peas, and onions.

2. Combine dressing and sugar. Spread on top of each layer, making sure it is well covered.

3. Chill for several hours. (It is best if made the night before.) Toss well before serving.

GLORIA WALL
Bread of Life
Pittsburg Freewill Baptist Church
Pittsburg, Illinois

PARTY VEGETABLE SALAD
Makes 10 to 12 servings

1 (10 OUNCE) PACKAGE FROZEN BROCCOLI SPEARS
1 (10 OUNCE) PACKAGE FROZEN FRENCH-STYLE
  GREEN BEANS
1 (10 OUNCE) PACKAGE FROZEN ASPARAGUS SPEARS
1 (10 OUNCE) PACKAGE FROZEN ARTICHOKE HEARTS
1 TABLESPOON ANCHOVY PASTE
1/2 CUP CREAM OR HALF & HALF
2 TABLESPOONS RED WINE VINEGAR
2 TABLESPOONS LEMON JUICE
1 GREEN BELL PEPPER, FINELY CHOPPED
1 CUCUMBER, FINELY CHOPPED
3/4 CUP PARSLEY, FINELY CHOPPED
1/4 CUP GREEN ONION, CHOPPED
1 CUP MAYONNAISE

1. Cook vegetables separately for half the required time indicated on the package.

2. Drain vegetables and cool on a cutting board. Cut into smaller pieces. Gently place in a large bowl and chill.

3. In a separate bowl, mix remaining ingredients for dressing. Chill.

4. Before serving, pour dressing over vegetables and toss.

MARIBELLE LEEPER
The Jubilee of Our Many Blessings Cookbook
Highland Park United Methodist Church
Dallas, Texas

CHICKEN PASTA SALAD WITH ROSEMARY DRESSING *Makes 4 servings*

ROSEMARY DRESSING:
1 LARGE CLOVE GARLIC, MINCED
1 TEASPOON SALT
$1/4$ TEASPOON BLACK PEPPER
$1/4$ CUP RED WINE VINEGAR
$1/2$ CUP OLIVE OIL
1 TEASPOON DRIED ROSEMARY OR 1 TABLESPOON
  FRESH ROSEMARY, MINCED

CHICKEN PASTA SALAD:
$2 1/2$ STRIPS CHICKEN, COOKED AND CUBED
2 CUPS COOKED PASTA, COLD
1 CUP ROASTED RED BELL PEPPER STRIPS
$1/2$ CUP RIPE OLIVES

1. Mix garlic, salt, pepper, and vinegar in salad bowl until the salt dissolves. Whisk in the oil and rosemary.

2. Add chicken, pasta, peppers, and olives. Toss to coat.

3. Cover and marinate in the refrigerator or overnight. Serve at room temperature.

To roast red bell peppers: Roast 2 medium red bell peppers on the grill, under the broiler, or with a fork over an open flame, turning often until the skin is charred. Place in a paper bag and let stand 5 minutes or until peel slips off easily. Yield: about 1 cup of strips.

TERESA CORDON
Thank Heaven for Homemade Cooks
Porter Memorial Baptist Church
Lexington, Kentucky

THICK CHILI SOUP
Makes 8 to 10 servings

2 POUNDS LEAN HAMBURGER
1/2 MEDIUM ONION, CHOPPED
1 MEDIUM RAW POTATO, GRATED
1 (15 OUNCE) CAN ARMOUR CHILI WITH BEANS
1 (15 OUNCE) CAN BROOKS CHILI BEANS
1/2 CUP KETCHUP
1 PINT TOMATO JUICE
3/4 CUP WATER
1 TABLESPOON SUGAR
1 TEASPOON WORCESTERSHIRE SAUCE
1 TEASPOON SALT
1/2 TEASPOON BLACK PEPPER

1. Brown hamburger and onion in large pan. Drain.

2. Add remaining ingredients and simmer for 2 hours.

LOTA FORD
Sharing Our Best
Third Baptist Church
Marion, Illinois

CREAM OF BROCCOLI SOUP
Makes 6 servings

4 CUPS WATER
3 CUPS BROCCOLI, CHOPPED
2 MEDIUM POTATOES, CHOPPED
2 MEDIUM ONIONS, CHOPPED
3 TABLESPOONS BUTTER OR MARGARINE
1/2 TEASPOON BASIL
1/2 TEASPOON BLACK PEPPER
2 CHICKEN-FLAVORED BOUILLON CUBES
1/2 TEASPOON DRIED THYME LEAVES
1/2 TEASPOON SALT
1 (13 OUNCE) CAN EVAPORATED MILK

1. Combine all ingredients, except milk, in a large pot. Bring to a boil.

2. Reduce heat and simmer for 30 minutes or until the broccoli is tender, stirring occasionally.

3. Spoon ⅓ of mixture into electric blender and blend for 20 seconds.

4. Repeat until all of mixture is blended.

5. Return to large pot, add milk, and simmer for 20 minutes.

VIRGIL COOPER (SUBMITTED BY LYDIS JONES)
Centennial Cookbook
First Baptist Church
Laurel, Mississippi

SUPER SIMPLE SOUP *Makes 6 servings*

2 CUPS CARROTS, CHOPPED
1 ½ CUPS POTATOES, CHOPPED
1 CUP ONION, CHOPPED
1 ½ CUPS WATER
1 POUND HAM, CUT IN SMALL PIECES
1 (10 OUNCE) PACKAGE FROZEN PEAS
1 CUP MILK
1 (10 ¾ OUNCE) CAN CREAM OF CELERY SOUP
2 CUPS CHEDDAR CHEESE, SHREDDED

1. In a 4½-quart soup pot combine carrots, potatoes, onion, and water. Bring to a boil; reduce heat. Cover and simmer until vegetables are just tender.

2. Add ham and peas.

3. Cover and cook 5 minutes more.

4. Stir in milk, soup, and cheese.

5. Cook and stir until heated through and cheese is melted.

LUELLA VOIGT
Feeding the Flock
First Baptist Church
Avon, South Dakota

SPINACH
STRAWBERRY SALAD *Makes 8 servings*

2 BUNCHES FRESH SPINACH, TORN
1 PINT FRESH STRAWBERRIES, RINSED AND SLICED
1/2 CUP SUGAR
1 1/2 TEASPOONS ONION, MINCED
1/4 TEASPOON WORCESTERSHIRE SAUCE
1/4 TEASPOON PAPRIKA
1/2 CUP VEGETABLE OIL
1/4 CUP CIDER VINEGAR
2 TABLESPOONS SESAME SEED
1 TABLESPOON POPPY SEED

1. Wash spinach and break into bite-size pieces. Place in a large salad bowl.

2. Add strawberries.

3. In a blender jar add sugar, onion, Worcestershire sauce, paprika, oil, and vinegar. Blend thoroughly; add seeds and blend to combine.

4. When ready, pour over the salad and serve.

DOROTHY JANE NEAL
First Baptist Church
Angleton, Texas

MISS SWEET
POTATO

ome October, the folks in my town have one thing on their minds, and that's the Miss Sweet Potato pageant and festival. All the eligible young women, which is defined loosely as nonmarried females between the ages of 17 and 34, compete year after year for the coveted title of Miss Sweet Potato. The talent competition is the same for everyone in that each young lady makes a sweet potato pie from scratch in the high school home economics kitchen while the judges observe and finally get to taste the finished product. There's also a congeniality award, "The Sweetest Potato," and a prize for the evening gown that most closely matches the orange hue of sweet potato meat.

This year, Tawny Trampler was gunning to win. She'd been third runner-up twice, and last year she was first runner-up, so she figured she was a shoo-in to sweep the pageant and cash in on the scholarship to Miss Wade's

Fashion Merchandising and Agricultural Sciences College. It had always been her dream to have a square-dance costume boutique with a feed store in the back. Miss Wade's was just about the only school that offered that kind of training.

Tawny had carefully analyzed all of her competition and counted Tiffany Tartlet as her only real rival. Not that Tiffany was prettier; it was those darn pie points that could give her the edge. Tawny had perfected her own pie recipe, but Tiffany's crust had a buttery flavor that was just delicious. Tawny was determined to discover just what Tiffany's secret was in order to cinch that crown.

As luck would have it, Tiffany and Tawny shared a dressing room during the pageant. One afternoon before rehearsal for the big dance finale, Tawny saw her opportunity to snoop through Tiffany's grocery sacks. When Tiffany was fixing her hair and could not see for the clouds of hairspray around her head, Tawny rummaged quickly through the sacks. Before the haze began to dissipate, Tawny seized upon the mysterious ingredient: disguised in a plain, brown wrapper was a tub of butter-flavored Crisco.

It was too late for Tawny to change her list of ingredients, so she figured she could create her own butter-flavored Crisco by mixing her plain Crisco with real butter. As she kneaded the butter into the lard, Tawny flashed a smug smile at Tiffany, never realizing the effect butter and lard have on press-on nail glue. As she handed her pie to the judges, she realized to her horror that she had lost three press-on nails at some point during the preparation of the pie.

Just then the sheriff spat out a Persimmon-Passion-painted nail while Miss Bundy, the Latin teacher, began to choke and gag on her piece of pie. Miss Bundy ended up at the hospital where a perfectly manicured nail was extracted from the roof of her mouth. Tawny received negative points for pie crust, but did get a few points for unique ingredients.

Tawny did not make the top ten finalists this year. She was devastated by the loss and has vowed never to eat another sweet potato as long as she lives. Tiffany won the competition hands down and is touring the county, making appearances and pies at every stop. Miss Tartlet will be enrolling at Miss Wade's next year and plans to become a spokesmodel for sweet potatoes.

WHEN THE ROLLS ARE DONE
UP YONDER, I'LL BE THERE
BREADS

 = "A piece of cake" (quick and easy)

A-Z LOAF   *Makes 2 large loaves*

3 CUPS ALL-PURPOSE FLOUR
1 TEASPOON SALT
1 TEASPOON BAKING SODA
3 TEASPOONS CINNAMON
$\frac{1}{2}$ TEASPOON BAKING POWDER
3 EGGS
1 CUP VEGETABLE OIL
2 CUPS SUGAR
2 CUPS A-Z (SEE FOLLOWING LIST)
3 TEASPOONS VANILLA EXTRACT
1 CUP NUTS, CHOPPED

Preheat oven to 350°.

1. Sift dry ingredients together. Set aside.

2. Beat eggs in a large bowl. Add oil and sugar. Cream well.

3. Add A-Z and vanilla.

4. Add dry ingredients. Mix well.

5. Blend in nuts.

6. Spoon into two well-greased and floured loaf pans.

7. Bake for 1 hour or until golden brown.

A-Z

Use one of the following or a mixture of the following to equal 2 cups, except as indicated:

APPLES, GRATED
APPLESAUCE
APRICOTS
BANANAS, MASHED
CARROTS, GRATED
CHERRIES, PITTED AND CHOPPED
COCONUT, FRESH GROUND

BREADS

DATES, PITTED AND FINELY CHOPPED
EGGPLANT, GROUND
FIGS, FINELY CHOPPED
GRAPES, SEEDLESS AND CHOPPED
HONEY (OMIT SUGAR)
LEMONS (USE ONLY $\frac{1}{2}$ CUP JUICE)
MARMALADE (OMIT 1 CUP SUGAR)
MINCEMEAT
ORANGES, CHOPPED
PEACHES, CANNED OR FRESH, CHOPPED
PEARS, CHOPPED
PEPPERMINT, CHOPPED
PINEAPPLE, CRUSHED AND DRAINED
PRUNES, CHOPPED (USE 1 CUP)
PUMPKIN, CANNED
RAISINS
RASPBERRIES, CHOPPED
RHUBARB, CHOPPED
STRAWBERRIES, FRESH OR FROZEN, WELL-DRAINED
SWEET POTATOES, GRATED COARSELY
TAPIOCA, COOKED
TOMATOES (USE ONLY $\frac{1}{2}$ CUP SUGAR)
YAMS, COOKED AND MASHED
YOGURT, PLAIN OR FLAVORED
ZUCCHINI, GRATED

BARBARA VAN GERPEN
First Baptist Church
Avon, South Dakota

PIE FILLING
COFFEE CAKE *Makes 10 servings*

1 STICK BUTTER, SOFTENED TO ROOM TEMPERATURE
1 CUP SUGAR
1 CUP SOUR CREAM
2 EGGS
1 TEASPOON VANILLA EXTRACT
2 CUPS ALL-PURPOSE FLOUR
1 1/2 TEASPOONS BAKING POWDER
1/2 TEASPOON BAKING SODA
1 (20 OUNCE) CAN PIE FILLING (APPLE, CHERRY, BLUEBERRY, OR APRICOT)

TOPPING:
1/4 CUP (1/2 STICK) MARGARINE OR BUTTER, MELTED
1/2 CUP ALL-PURPOSE FLOUR
1/2 CUP CHOPPED NUTS
1/2 CUP SUGAR
1 TABLESPOON CINNAMON

Preheat oven to 350°.

1. Mix butter, sugar, sour cream, eggs, and vanilla. Stir until well blended.

2. Sift together the dry ingredients and combine with the first mixture.

3. Spread half the batter into a greased 9- x 13-inch pan. Top with pie filling.

4. Combine topping ingredients. Spread half of mixture over pie filling.

5. Repeat layers.

6. Bake for 45 minutes or until golden brown.

JANE GRAY
Zion Lutheran Church
Cottage Grove, Minnesota

OATMEAL BREAD *Makes 4 loaves*

2 CUPS QUICK-COOKING OATS
2 CUPS WHOLE-WHEAT FLOUR
1 SCANT CUP BROWN SUGAR, NOT PACKED
2 TABLESPOONS SALT
4 TABLESPOONS MARGARINE OR BUTTER
5 CUPS WATER, DIVIDED
2 ($\frac{1}{4}$ OUNCE) PACKAGES ACTIVE DRY YEAST
8 TO 10 CUPS WHITE ALL-PURPOSE FLOUR

1. Combine oats, wheat flour, sugar, salt, and butter in a large bowl.

2. Pour 4 cups of boiling water over the combined ingredients. Stir and let cool.

3. Dissolve yeast in 1 cup warm water and let bubble.

4. Add yeast mixture to lukewarm batter.

5. Stir in white flour a little at a time until mixture is a stiff consistency.

6. Turn onto floured board. Knead for 15 minutes.

7. Place into greased bowl, cover, and let rise in a warm place until doubled.

8. Punch dough down and form into 4 loaves.

9. Place into greased loaf pans for second rising (until doubled). Preheat oven to 350°.

10. Bake for 40 minutes. Cool out of pans on wire racks.

CAROL HOLTZ-MARTIN
First Baptist Church
Macedon, New York

YEAST ROLLS *Makes 3 dozen*

1 CUP BOILING WATER
1 CUP SOLID SHORTENING
1 CUP SUGAR
1 ½ TEASPOONS SALT
2 EGGS, BEATEN
2 (1 OUNCE) PACKAGES ACTIVE DRY YEAST
1 CUP LUKEWARM WATER
6 CUPS ALL-PURPOSE FLOUR

1. Combine boiling water, shortening, sugar, and salt.

2. Blend well and cool.

3. Add eggs.

4. Sprinkle yeast into lukewarm water. Stir until dissolved.

5. Combine with egg mixture.

6. Blend in flour a little at a time until well mixed. Cover and refrigerate for 4 hours.

7. Spray a muffin tin with cooking spray. Roll the dough into balls and place balls in the muffin tin.

8. Let rise for 3 hours. Preheat oven to 400°.

9. Bake for 12 to 15 minutes.

This dough will keep a week to 10 days and may be used as needed.

MARGARET LONG (RECIPE USED BY MRS. DENKMAN)
Second Baptist Church
Memphis, Tennessee

BREAD IN A JAR *Makes 8 pints*

⅔ CUP SOLID SHORTENING
2 ⅔ CUPS SUGAR
4 EGGS
2 CUPS CANNED PUMPKIN
⅔ CUP WATER
3 ⅓ CUPS ALL-PURPOSE FLOUR
½ TEASPOON BAKING POWDER
2 TEASPOONS BAKING SODA
1 ½ TEASPOONS SALT
1 TEASPOON CINNAMON
1 TEASPOON GROUND CLOVES
⅔ CUP NUTS

Preheat oven to 325°.

1. Cream shortening and sugar until blended.

2. Beat in eggs, pumpkin, and water.

3. Sift together flour, baking powder, soda, salt, and spices. Add to the pumpkin mixture.

4. Stir in the nuts.

5. Pour mixture into 8 well-greased, wide-mouth jars, filling each ⅔ full.

6. Place jars on a baking sheet in the oven. Bake for 30 to 35 minutes.

7. When the bread is done, remove one jar at a time and wipe the jar rim with a clean, damp cloth. Place the lid on the jar, then screw the cap on tightly. The heat will vacuum seal the jar, and the bread will keep for up to 1 year.

DOTTIE VINCENT
Midway United Missionary Baptist Church
Lindseyville, Kentucky

BROCCOLI CORN BREAD *Makes 8 servings*

4 EGGS
2 (8½ OUNCE) BOXES CORN BREAD MIX
1½ CUPS COTTAGE CHEESE
1½ STICKS BUTTER OR MARGARINE, MELTED
1 MEDIUM ONION, CHOPPED
1 (10 OUNCE) PACKAGE CHOPPED BROCCOLI,
   THAWED AND DRAINED

Preheat oven to 400°.

1. Beat eggs and add corn bread mix, cottage cheese, butter, and chopped onion. Stir to combine.

2. Add broccoli and mix gently.

3. Pour mixture into a 9- x 13-inch pan that has been sprayed with cooking spray.

4. Bake for 20 to 25 minutes. (It will be on the soft side.) To serve, cut into squares.

MILDRED MCALLISTER
Centennial Cookbook
Polytechnic United Methodist Church
Fort Worth, Texas

BUTTERSCOTCH-GRANOLA COFFEE CAKE *Makes 10 to 12 servings*

1¼ CUPS ALL-PURPOSE FLOUR
½ CUP SUGAR
¾ CUP SOUR CREAM
½ CUP (1 STICK) BUTTER, SOFTENED TO ROOM
   TEMPERATURE
¾ TEASPOON BAKING POWDER
½ TEASPOON SALT
½ TEASPOON ORANGE PEEL
3 EGGS
1 CUP GRANOLA

FILLING:
½ OF ONE (6 OUNCE) PACKAGE BUTTERSCOTCH-
 FLAVORED MORSELS
½ CUP CHOPPED NUTS
½ TEASPOON GROUND CINNAMON

GLAZE:
⅓ OF ONE (6 OUNCE) PACKAGE BUTTERSCOTCH-
 FLAVORED MORSELS
1 TABLESPOON BUTTER
2 TEASPOONS HALF & HALF

Preheat oven to 350°.

1. Mix together the first 8 ingredients.

2. Stir in the granola.

3. In a separate bowl, prepare filling by mixing ½ package of morsels, nuts, and cinnamon.

4. Spread half of batter into an oiled, 9-inch square pan. Sprinkle with filling.

5. Top with remaining batter.

6. Bake until the crust is golden brown (about 30 minutes). Cool completely.

7. Glaze: Heat ⅓ package of morsels, butter, and half & half over medium heat until smooth.

8. Drizzle coffee cake with glaze and top with additional nuts, if desired.

MARIANNE AND CHRIS DEPTOLA
DREW DEPTOLA
Christ Evangelical Lutheran Church
Jeffersontown, Kentucky

SWEET POTATO
BISCUITS   *Makes 18 to 20 biscuits*

1 ½ CUPS ALL-PURPOSE FLOUR
¾ TABLESPOON BAKING POWDER
1 TEASPOON BAKING SODA
½ TEASPOON NUTMEG
½ TEASPOON SALT
6 TABLESPOONS BUTTER
1 ½ CUPS SWEET POTATO, COOKED AND MASHED
⅓ CUP BUTTERMILK

Preheat oven to 425°.

1. Combine dry ingredients in a bowl. Mix well.

2. Cut in butter until mixture resembles coarse crumbs.

3. Combine sweet potatoes with buttermilk.

4. Stir into dry ingredients, blending to make a soft dough. Turn out onto a lightly floured surface. Knead 4 or 5 times or just enough to form a ball.

5. Roll dough to about ⅓-inch thickness. Cut into 2-inch rounds using a biscuit cutter dipped in flour.

6. Place on a lightly oiled baking sheet. Bake for about 15 minutes or until puffy and lightly browned.

DOLORES ULRICH
Thank Heaven for Homemade Cooks
Porter Memorial Baptist Church
Lexington, Kentucky

ONION BREAD   *Makes 8 to 10 servings*

1 (1 OUNCE) PACKAGE ACTIVE DRY YEAST
¼ CUP WATER
4 CUPS ALL-PURPOSE FLOUR, DIVIDED
¼ CUP SUGAR
1 ½ TEASPOONS SALT

½ CUP MILK
¼ CUP (½ STICK) BUTTER, SOFTENED TO
  ROOM TEMPERATURE
1 EGG

FILLING:
¼ CUP (½ STICK) BUTTER
1 CUP ONION, FINELY CHOPPED
2 TEASPOONS PARMESAN CHEESE, GRATED
1 TEASPOON POPPY SEED
1 TEASPOON GARLIC SALT
1 TEASPOON PAPRIKA

1. Dissolve yeast in water. Add half of flour and the next five ingredients.

2. Beat the batter with a mixer on low speed until ingredients are well blended (about three minutes).

3. Gradually add the rest of the flour by hand to form a soft dough. Cover the bowl with a damp towel, and let it rise in a warm place until doubled (about 45 to 60 minutes).

4. Roll out the dough to form a 12- x 18-inch rectangle.

5. To prepare the filling: Melt the butter and stir in the remaining ingredients. Spread the filling onto the dough.

6. Cut the bread lengthwise to make three 4- x 18-inch strips.

7. Roll up the strips lengthwise, and seal the edges and ends. Braid the strips on a greased cookie sheet. Cover the bread and let rise again 45 to 60 minutes or until doubled.

8. Preheat oven to 350°. Bake for 30 to 35 minutes.

CARLA BEDNAR
Keeping the Feast
Saint George's Episcopal Church
Austin, Texas

WHOLE-WHEAT QUICK BREAD
Makes 2 loaves

1 EGG, BEATEN
2 CUPS BUTTERMILK
3 TABLESPOONS MOLASSES OR HONEY
1 1/2 TABLESPOONS BUTTER, MELTED
1 TEASPOON BAKING SODA
1 TEASPOON SALT
2 CUPS WHOLE-WHEAT FLOUR
1 TEASPOON BAKING POWDER
1/2 CUP NUTS (OPTIONAL)
1/2 CUP RAISINS

Preheat oven to 400°.

1. Combine egg, buttermilk, molasses, and melted butter.

2. Combine the dry ingredients. Blend into egg mixture.

3. Stir in nuts and raisins. Spoon batter into two greased loaf pans.

4. Bake for 1 hour.

PENNY LINDSEY
Sharing Our Best
Midway United Missionary Church
Lindseyville, Kentucky

 # BUSY DAY BISCUITS
Makes 1 dozen

1 CUP SOUR CREAM
1 STICK MARGARINE OR BUTTER, MELTED
2 CUPS BISQUICK

Preheat oven to 350°.

1. Combine all ingredients well. Drop dough into small, ungreased muffin tins.

2. Bake for 10 minutes or until lightly golden.

NAOMI THOMPSON
Sharing Our Best
Midway United Missionary Church
Lindseyville, Kentucky

CRANBERRY MUFFINS *Makes 1 dozen*

2 CUPS ALL-PURPOSE FLOUR
1 CUP SUGAR
1 1/2 TEASPOONS BAKING POWDER
1/2 TEASPOON BAKING SODA
2 TEASPOONS ORANGE PEEL, GRATED
1 1/2 TEASPOONS NUTMEG
1 TEASPOON CINNAMON
1/2 TEASPOON GINGER
1/2 CUP SOLID SHORTENING
3/4 CUP ORANGE JUICE
1 TABLESPOON VANILLA EXTRACT
2 EGGS, SLIGHTLY BEATEN
1 1/2 CUPS CRANBERRIES
1 1/2 CUPS WALNUTS

Preheat oven to 350°.

1. In a medium bowl mix flour, sugar, baking powder, baking soda, orange peel, and spices.

2. Cut in the shortening with a pastry blender or fork.

3. Stir in juice, vanilla, and eggs.

4. Fold in cranberries and walnuts.

5. Spoon into a well-greased or paper-lined 2½-inch muffin cups.

6. Bake for 15 to 20 minutes or until browned.

MONA BRASHEAR
Food for My Household
Audubon Baptist Church
Louisville, Kentucky

BUBBLE LOAF *Makes 1 large loaf*

1 (2½ OUNCES) PACKAGE FROZEN BRIDGEFORD
   PARKERHOUSE ROLLS
2 (3 OUNCE) PACKAGES BUTTERSCOTCH PUDDING
½ CUP BROWN SUGAR, FIRMLY PACKED
2 TEASPOONS CINNAMON
½ CUP CHOPPED NUTS
1 STICK BUTTER, MELTED

1. Butter or spray a bundt pan.

2. Arrange half of package of rolls in the pan.

3. Mix together the dry ingredients. Sprinkle half of mixture over rolls.

4. Sprinkle with half the nuts. Add half of melted butter.

5. Repeat for second layer with remaining rolls, dry ingredients, nuts, and butter.

6. Let rise in a warm place for 3 to 4 hours. (I make this the night before, cover, and put it on the counter or in a cold oven until the next morning.) Preheat oven to 375°.

7. Bake for 25 to 30 minutes. (May need to cover top with foil during last 5 to 10 minutes to prevent overbrowning on top.)

JUDITH BLACKLEDGE
Cenntennial Cookbook
First Baptist Church
Laurel, Mississippi

SAUSAGE BREAD *Makes 2 dozen*

1 POUND HOT BULK PORK SAUSAGE, BROWNED,
   DRAINED, AND CRUMBLED
1 CUP HOT CHEESE, GRATED
1 (16 OUNCE) CAN CREAM STYLE CORN
¾ CUP CORN MEAL
½ CUP ALL-PURPOSE FLOUR
2 EGGS, LIGHTLY BEATEN
½ TEASPOON SALT
½ TEASPOON BAKING POWDER

Preheat oven to 400°.

1. In a large bowl, mix together all ingredients.

2. Spray a muffin tin or cornstick pan with cooking spray and fill each compartment ⅔ full.

3. Bake for 30 minutes.

LOUISE OLDS
Evergreen Cookbook
Evergreen Baptist Church
Frankfort, Kentucky

TEDDY TERROR

The Sapwaters have but one chant for their annual family reunions— What are we gonna eat? Planning begins about six months out with each family canning, preserving, killing, hooking, spearing, freezing, and preparing. Elmo and Sarah Sapwater have six sons and three daughters, who have each married and produced fifteen grandchildren to make a whopping thirty-five people to feed morning, noon, and night for a solid week each summer.

When they're not eating, the family sits around thinking up new tricks to play on each other. Grandpa Elmo is a favorite target because he's gotten a bit crotchety in his old age and seems to enjoy yelling at the grandkids to stay off the grass. This pretty much confuses the children since there's nothing but grass around the log cabins they rent for the reunion. Grandpa's hearing and eyesight aren't what they used to be, but his mind is as sharp as a steel trap, so it takes a lot of planning to fool him.

Grandpa was always trying to scare the grandkids. He would tell them long stories about ferocious big brown bears that carried children off to their dens and tore them from limb to limb, savoring them for their supper. Of course, Grandpa failed to mention that there hadn't been a bear spotted in this neck of the woods since the 1930s and that he personally had never seen a bear up close in his life.

The idea came to the oldest son, Delmont, when he was watching his daughter unload her favorite stuffed animal, a six-foot-tall brown teddy bear named Ralph, from the trunk of the car. He quickly conferred with his brothers and sisters, and a plan was hatched. The next morning at breakfast he set the teddy bear about thirty feet away from the picnic tables, propped against a big oak tree on its hind legs. About the time everybody had settled down to a big plateful of cheese grits and sausage-rice casserole, Delmont called his dog, Dufus, over. Dufus was aptly named and would bark at just about anything. Delmont whispered the magic words "squirrel in the tree," and Dufus took off running and yelping at the oak tree where Ralph was standing.

That's when the fun began. Darrin and Darrell, the twins, began hollering, "Daddy, there's a bear over there! Get your shotgun. We'll have bear stew for dinner!" The grandkids started shrieking and jumping up on the picnic tables. Grandma ran in the cabin and brought Grandpa his gun, screaming, "Don't shoot Dufus! Don't shoot Dufus!"

Delmont had wisely emptied Grandpa's gun of all the bullets, which Elmo soon discovered. "We'll have to wrestle him, Daddy" said Dodie, and all the sons chimed in, "Yeah, we can kill him with our bare hands. Come on Daddy, let's go."

"Are you kids crazy? Have you lost your minds? That bear could kill every one of you!" Grandpa said as he continued to eye the bear. "We can do it. Let's rush him!" the sons said as they ran toward the bear. As they reached the bear, Delbert grabbed him around the neck and gave an Academy Award performance of pretending to wrestle with the bear. From time to time one of the other brothers would join in. After about five minutes of rolling around on the ground, the men could not hold in the laughter any longer. "Gotcha, Daddy!" they called in unison as they brought Elmo the "dead" bear.

Elmo tried to claim that he knew it all along, but nobody believed him. Every year after that Ralph would show up at some meal, in a tree or under the table, and Delmont would wrestle the bear for the youngest kids' excitement and to remind Grandpa how they had fooled him.

JUST AS I HAM

MAIN
DISHES

CHICKEN AND ARTICHOKE CASSEROLE *Makes 4 to 6 servings*

$\frac{1}{4}$ POUND (1 STICK) BUTTER
3 TABLESPOONS FLOUR
1 CUP MILK
$\frac{3}{4}$ CUP CHICKEN BROTH
1 TEASPOON SALT
1 (8 OUNCE) CAN TOMATO SAUCE
$\frac{1}{8}$ TEASPOON GROUND RED PEPPER
$\frac{1}{2}$ CLOVE GARLIC, CHOPPED
$\frac{1}{8}$ POUND (2 OUNCES) SHARP CHEDDAR CHEESE,
   GRATED
$3\frac{1}{2}$ OUNCES SWISS CHEESE, DICED
$1\frac{1}{2}$ (4 OUNCE) CANS MUSHROOMS, DRAINED
3 CHICKEN BREASTS, COOKED AND HALVED
1 (16 OUNCE) CAN ARTICHOKES
$\frac{1}{2}$ CUP BREAD CRUMBS

Preheat oven to 350°.

1. Melt butter in small pan. Whisk in flour. Add milk and stir until thickened.

2. Add broth, salt, tomato sauce, pepper, garlic, and cheeses. Continue stirring until blended and thickened. Stir in mushrooms.

3. Layer chicken, sauce, and artichokes alternately in baking dish.

4. Top with bread crumbs.

5. Bake until bubbly.

PATSY NEAL
Viands and Vittles
Forest Hills United Methodist Church
Brentwood, Tennessee

HEAVENLY MEATLOAF   *Makes 8 to 10 servings*

2 EGGS, BEATEN
2 TEASPOONS SALT
3 SLICES BREAD, CUBED
⅔ CUP MILK
¼ TEASPOON BLACK PEPPER
⅔ CUP ONION, FINELY CHOPPED
⅔ CUP CARROTS, SHREDDED
1½ CUPS MILD CHEDDAR CHEESE, SHREDDED
2 POUNDS GROUND BEEF

GLAZE:
¼ CUP BROWN SUGAR, FIRMLY PACKED
1 TABLESPOON MUSTARD
¼ CUP KETCHUP

Preheat oven to 350°.

1. Beat eggs, salt, bread cubes, milk, and pepper with a beater until mushy.

2. Add onion, carrots, cheese, and ground beef. Place in a loaf pan.

3. Bake for 1 hour and 15 minutes.

4. Mix the glaze ingredients. Spoon onto the meatloaf and bake for an additional 15 minutes.

JAN LANGE
Heavenly Creations
Zion Lutheran Church
Cottage Grove, Minnesota

HAM LOAF   *Makes 8 servings*

1 POUND GROUND BEEF
$\frac{1}{2}$ POUND GROUND LEAN PORK
$\frac{1}{2}$ POUND GROUND CURED HAM
1 EGG, BEATEN
$\frac{1}{2}$ CUP MILK
1 TABLESPOON ONION JUICE
1 TEASPOON WORCESTERSHIRE SAUCE
$\frac{1}{2}$ CUP CRACKERS, FINELY CRUMBLED
1 $\frac{1}{2}$ TEASPOONS SALT
$\frac{1}{4}$ TEASPOON BLACK PEPPER

SAUCE:
1 CUP HEAVY CREAM
$\frac{1}{4}$ CUP HORSERADISH
DASH OF SALT

Preheat oven to 350°.

1. Mix the meats together in a large bowl.

2. In a separate bowl. Mix the next 7 ingredients.

3. Add this mixture to the meats and mix together thoroughly. Form the mixture into a loaf and place into a lightly oiled loaf pan.

4. Bake for 1½ hours.

5. Combine sauce ingredients in a small saucepan. Warm slowly, stirring constantly. Pour over ham loaf or serve on the side.

ANNE REED
Keeping the Feast
Saint George Episcopal Church
Austin, Texas

GARDEN PATCH PIE   *Makes 4 to 6 servings*

1 POUND LEAN GROUND BEEF
½ CUP INSTANT MASHED POTATOES
¼ CUP KETCHUP
¼ CUP ONION, CHOPPED
1 TABLESPOON WORCESTERSHIRE SAUCE
½ TEASPOON SALT
¼ TEASPOON BLACK PEPPER
1 EGG, SLIGHTLY BEATEN
1 CUP FROZEN MIXED VEGETABLES

TOPPING:
1 CUP WATER
3 TABLESPOONS BUTTER
1½ CUPS INSTANT MASHED POTATOES
½ CUP MILK
½ CUP CHEDDAR CHEESE, SHREDDED
PAPRIKA

Preheat oven to 350°.

1. Brown ground beef and drain.

2. Combine beef and the next 8 ingredients in a 7- x 11-inch pan. Stir to combine.

3. In a small bowl, mix the topping ingredients, except paprika. Spread over the ground beef mixture.

4. Bake until the potatoes are slightly browned.

5. Sprinkle with paprika before serving.

STACY AND JOLENE VALEU
Favorite Recipes from Our Best Cooks
Christian Bible Church
Springfield, Illinois

CREOLE TURKEY CASSEROLE *Makes 8 servings*

2 MEDIUM ONIONS, FINELY CHOPPED
1 GREEN BELL PEPPER, FINELY CHOPPED
⅓ CUP BACON DRIPPINGS
1 (8 OUNCE) CAN MUSHROOMS, UNDRAINED
1 (14½ OUNCE) CAN TOMATOES, UNDRAINED AND CHOPPED
1 (8 OUNCE) CAN TOMATO SAUCE
1 (6 OUNCE) CAN TOMATO PASTE
¼ CUP APPLE JUICE
1 TABLESPOON GARLIC, MINCED
DASH OF GROUND BLACK PEPPER
DASH OF HOT SAUCE
DASH OF WORCESTERSHIRE SAUCE
4 CUPS RICE, COOKED
3 CUPS TURKEY, COOKED AND CUBED
GREEN BELL PEPPER RINGS
FRESH PARSLEY SPRIGS

Preheat oven to 350°.

1. In a large skillet, sauté onion and green pepper in the bacon drippings until tender.

2. Add the next 9 ingredients and bring to a boil.

3. Reduce heat, cover, and simmer for 12 minutes.

4. Spoon rice evenly in the bottom of a 9- x 13-inch baking dish. Top with turkey.

5. Spoon sauce over the turkey. Bake, uncovered, for 15 minutes or until thoroughly heated.

6. Garnish with green pepper rings and parsley.

MARTHA MILNER
Moscow United Methodist Church
Moscow, Kansas

CRANBERRY CHICKEN   *Makes 6 servings*

6 CHICKEN BREASTS
1 CAN WHOLE CRANBERRIES
1 (8 OUNCE) BOTTLE FRENCH DRESSING
1 (1 TO 1½ OUNCE) ENVELOPE DRY ONION
   SOUP MIX

Preheat oven to 350°.

1. Place chicken in a 9- x 13-inch baking dish.

2. Mix remaining ingredients and pour over the chicken.

3. Cover and bake for 1 hour. Remove cover and bake 20 minutes longer.

JEWELL LOYD
Desoto Baptist Church
Desoto, Illinois

SHRIMP GUMBO   *Makes 2 gallons*

1 POUND GROUND BEEF
½ POUND SAUSAGE, GROUND
2 CUPS GREEN BELL PEPPER, CHOPPED
1 CUP ONION, CHOPPED
1 CLOVE GARLIC, MINCED
¼ TEASPOON GROUND RED PEPPER
1 TEASPOON DRIED CELERY FLAKES
1 TEASPOON SALT
1 TEASPOON BLACK PEPPER
1 (10¾ OUNCE) CAN CREAM OF CHICKEN SOUP
1 (10¾ OUNCE) CAN CREAM OF ONION SOUP
1 (16 OUNCE) CAN BLACK-EYED PEAS
1 (16 OUNCE) CAN CORN
TABASCO SAUCE TO TASTE
12 OUNCES SHRIMP, PEELED AND CLEANED
½ CUP RAW RICE

1. Combine the first 5 ingredients in a 12-quart kettle. Cook over low heat until browned. Drain fat.

2. Add the remaining ingredients, except shrimp and rice, to the mixture, adding enough water to just cover the mixture. Maintain the liquid level by adding water as needed.

3. Add rice and simmer an additional 30 minutes.

4. About 5 to 6 minutes before serving, add the shrimp. Make sure the shrimp is opaque before serving. (Gumbo can be made ahead and frozen.)

DARRELL DIXON
Favorite Recipes from Our Best Cooks
Dorrisville Baptist Church
Dorrisville, Illinois

HAMBURGER PIE *Makes 6 servings*

1 ½ POUNDS GROUND BEEF
1 ONION, CHOPPED
1 TEASPOON SALT
½ TEASPOON BLACK PEPPER
1 ROUNDED TEASPOON CHILI POWDER
¼ TEASPOON GARLIC SALT
1 (10¾ OUNCE) CAN TOMATO SOUP (NO WATER)
1 (16 OUNCE) CAN RANCH STYLE BEANS
2 CUPS POTATOES, GRATED
2 CUPS CHEESE, GRATED
1 (8½ OUNCE) BOX JIFFY CORN BREAD MIX

Preheat oven to 350°.

1. Brown beef and onion, drain off fat.

2. Add salt, pepper, chili powder, garlic salt, soup, and beans.

3. Place in a 7- x 11-inch or 9- x 13-inch baking pan.

4. Top with a layer of grated potatoes and a layer of grated cheese.

5. Mix cornbread according to the directions on the box, but add extra milk to make the batter a little thinner.

6. Pour over the top of the cheese.

7. Bake for 35 to 40 minutes or until the cornbread is lightly browned.

MARION WHITENER
Seasoned with Love
Cornerstone Assembly of God Church
Bethany, Oklahoma

HAM AND BROCCOLI ROLL-UPS *Makes 4 servings*

2 AMERICAN CHEESE SLICES
8 HAM SLICES
8 BROCCOLI SPEARS, PARTIALLY COOKED
1 (10¾ OUNCE) CAN CREAM OF MUSHROOM SOUP
1 CUP SOUR CREAM
1 TEASPOON MUSTARD
½ CUP MINCED ONION
½ CUP GREEN BELL PEPPER, CHOPPED
1 (2 OUNCE) JAR PIMIENTOS, CHOPPED

Preheat oven to 350°.

1. Place ¼ slice of cheese on each ham slice. Add 1 broccoli spear, roll up and secure with toothpick. Place in baking dish. Repeat with remaining cheese, ham, and broccoli.

2. Combine remaining ingredients to make the sauce. Pour over the roll-ups.

3. Bake, covered, for 35 to 40 minutes.

KARLA AND MARK UNKENHOLZ
Jubilee of Our Many Blessings Cookbook
Highland Park United Methodist Church
Dallas, Texas

CHICKEN WAIKIKI BEACH *Makes 4 servings*

4 LARGE CHICKEN BREASTS
⅓ CUP SALAD DRESSING (RANCH OR FRENCH)
½ CUP ALL-PURPOSE FLOUR
VEGETABLE OIL
1 TEASPOON SALT
¼ TEASPOON BLACK PEPPER

SAUCE:
1 (20 OUNCE) CAN PINEAPPLE CHUNKS
1 CUP SUGAR
2 TABLESPOONS CORNSTARCH
¾ CUP CIDER VINEGAR
1 TABLESPOON SOY SAUCE
¼ TEASPOON GINGER
1 CHICKEN BOUILLON CUBE
1 LARGE GREEN BELL PEPPER, CUT IN ¼-INCH
    THICK RINGS

1. Coat the chicken with favorite salad dressing (Ranch or French suggested), then dip and coat in flour.

2. Brown in hot oil on all sides. Drain; season with salt and pepper. Place in casserole dish. Preheat oven to 350°.

3. Drain the syrup from the pineapple. Add water to the syrup to make 1¼ cups liquid.

4. In a small saucepan combine the sugar, cornstarch, pineapple liquid, vinegar, soy sauce, ginger, and bouillon.

5. Bring to a boil, stirring constantly. Boil 2 minutes. Pour over the chicken.

6. Bake, uncovered, for 30 minutes. Add pineapple chunks and green pepper and bake 30 minutes longer.

HOPE RIDLEY
The Cupboard
Congregational Church of San Mateo
San Mateo, California

MARINATED ROAST *Makes 8 servings*

1 (3 TO 4 POUND) ROAST
2 TABLESPOONS VEGETABLE OIL
2 CLOVES GARLIC, MINCED
1/4 TEASPOON DRY MUSTARD
1/2 TEASPOON PEPPER
1 TABLESPOON VINEGAR
1 CUP DR. PEPPER
2 TABLESPOONS KETCHUP
1 1/2 TEASPOONS SALT
2 TABLESPOONS SOY SAUCE

1. Place roast in a shallow dish.

2. Place oil in a skillet and sauté the garlic. Add remaining ingredients and mix well.

3. Pour mixture over the roast. Place in the refrigerator for 6 to 24 hours; turn the roast several times so it is well marinated. Preheat oven to 325°.

4. Line roasting pan with heavy aluminum foil. Place roast on the foil, bending the foil up around the roast, leaving the top open.

5. Pour the marinade over the roast.

6. Roast for 2 1/2 hours.

H. STEWART
Butter'n' Love Recipes
Little Dove Church of Regular Baptist
Sassafras, Kentucky

CHICKEN AND DRESSING CASSEROLE *Makes 4 to 6 servings*

1 PACKAGE PREPARED DRESSING (PEPPERIDGE FARM)
2 TABLESPOONS BUTTER, MELTED
1 WHOLE CHICKEN BAKED OR BOILED AND CUT OFF
  THE BONE
1 (10¾ OUNCE) CAN CREAM OF CHICKEN SOUP
2 CUPS CHICKEN BROTH

Preheat oven to 350°.

1. Spray a 9- x 13-inch casserole dish with cooking spray.

2. In a separate bowl, combine dressing mix with melted butter, stirring thoroughly to combine. Spoon half of dressing mixture in the casserole dish.

3. Add layers of chicken and cream of chicken soup. Repeat layers.

4. Top with remaining dressing and pour chicken broth over the casserole.

5. Bake for 1 hour.

MARTHA BAIN RICE
Cooking with Love
Glen's Creek Baptist Church
Versailles, Kentucky

BARBECUED POT ROAST *Makes 8 to 10 servings*

2 (10¾ OUNCE) CANS TOMATO SOUP
1 (14 OUNCE) BOTTLE OF KETCHUP
½ CUP BROWN SUGAR, FIRMLY PACKED
3 TABLESPOONS MOLASSES
1 TEASPOON DRY MUSTARD
1 TEASPOON SALT
1 TEASPOON BLACK PEPPER
3 TABLESPOONS LIQUID SMOKE

1 SMALL ONION, SLICED AND BROWNED IN BUTTER
1 (4 TO 5 POUND) BEEF ROAST

Preheat oven to 300°.

1. Simmer all ingredients, except meat, for 30 minutes.

2. Cook pot roast for 2 to 3 hours or until it begins to shred easily. When roast is done, shred it into a baking dish.

3. Pour the barbecue sauce over the shredded roast.

4. Bake in a 250° oven for 30 minutes.

MRS. WILLIAM F. HARRINGTON
St. Andrews Episcopal Church
Clear Lake, Iowa

SAUSAGE-RICE CASSEROLE   *Makes 10 to 12 servings*

1 POUND SAUSAGE
1 CUP UNCOOKED RICE
1 CUP ONION, CHOPPED
1 CUP CELERY, DICED
2 (10¾ OUNCE) CANS CREAM OF CHICKEN SOUP
2 (10¾ OUNCE) CANS CREAM OF MUSHROOM SOUP
1 SOUP CAN OF WATER

Preheat oven to 325°.

1. Brown sausage in a skillet.

2. Combine the remaining ingredients with the sausage.

3. Pour into a 9- x 13-inch casserole dish. Bake for 1 hour.

PATRICIA S. MAGILL
St. James Episcopal Church
Springfield, Missouri

CRISPY OVEN-FRIED CHICKEN *Makes 4 servings*

½ CUP (1 STICK) BUTTER
1 TEASPOON SALT OR ONION-SEASONED SALT
½ TEASPOON BLACK PEPPER
2 CUPS RICE KRISPIES CEREAL, CRUSHED
1 (3 POUND) BROILER-FRYER CHICKEN, CUT UP

Preheat oven to 350°.

1. Melt butter. Add salt and pepper.

2. Put cereal in a plastic bag and crush until fine.

3. Dip pieces of chicken in butter. Roll in crumbs.

4. Place chicken, bone side down, on a shallow, foil-lined pan.

5. Bake for 1 hour. Do not turn chicken.

MYRA WEBBER
St. Margaret's Episcopal Church
Belfast, Maine

TURKEY A LA KING CASSEROLE *Makes 6 servings*

4 OUNCES MEDIUM-SIZE NOODLES
1 (10¾ OUNCE) CAN CREAM OF CHICKEN SOUP
1 CUP MILK
1 TEASPOON SALT
1½ CUPS AMERICAN CHEESE, GRATED
2 CUPS LEFTOVER TURKEY, DICED
1 CUP CELERY, DICED
¼ CUP GREEN BELL PEPPER, DICED
¼ CUP PIMIENTO, DICED
1 CUP SLIVERED ALMONDS, DIVIDED
BREAD CRUMBS

1. Cook noodles as directed on package. Drain. Preheat oven to 350°.

2. Combine soup, milk, and salt. Cook over low heat, stirring constantly.

3. Add cheese and stir until melted.

4. Add turkey, celery, green pepper, pimiento, and ½ cup almonds. Mix thoroughly.

5. Put in a greased casserole dish. Top with crumbs and remaining almonds.

6. Bake, uncovered, for 45 minutes.

MRS. MARSHAL JAMES
St. Andrews Episcopal Church
Polson, Montana

MARYLAND CRAB CASSEROLE *Makes 8 servings*

3 TEASPOONS WORCESTERSHIRE SAUCE
1 TEASPOON VINEGAR
1 TEASPOON DRY MUSTARD
1 CUP EVAPORATED MILK
½ CUP (1 STICK) BUTTER
3 TABLESPOONS GREEN BELL PEPPER, DICED
1 POUND CRABMEAT, CLEANED AND PICKED OVER
1 CUP BREAD CRUMBS
SALT AND PEPPER TO TASTE

Preheat oven to 375°.

1. Combine Worcestershire sauce, vinegar, mustard, and milk. Set aside.

2. Melt butter in a large saucepan. Add green pepper and sauté for 2 minutes.

3. Reduce heat and add milk mixture.

4. Add crabmeat and allow mixture to bubble.

5. Add bread crumbs, salt, and pepper. Place in casserole dish.

6. Bake for 15 minutes or until brown.

MRS. JOHN FRED MILES
St Luke's Episcopal Church
Seaford, Delaware

BEEF BAKE
WITH DUMPLINGS *Makes 8 servings*

2 (1½ POUND) CANS BEEF STEW
1½ CUPS ALL-PURPOSE FLOUR, SIFTED
3 TABLESPOONS BAKING POWDER
¼ TEASPOON SALT
2 TEASPOONS POPPY SEED
1 TEASPOON CELERY SEED
½ TEASPOON MINCED ONION
3 TABLESPOONS VEGETABLE OIL
¾ CUP MILK
3 TABLESPOONS BUTTER, MELTED
⅔ CUP COARSE BREAD CRUMBS

Preheat oven to 375°.

1. Pour beef stew into a 2½-quart casserole or 9- x 9-inch baking dish.

2. Sift together flour, baking powder, and salt. Add poppy seed, celery seed, and onion.

3. Add oil and milk. Stir until moistened.

4. Mix butter and bread crumbs. Drop flour mixture by rounded teaspoon-fuls into bread crumbs. Roll to coat with crumbs.

5. Place on top of stew. Bake, uncovered, for 45 to 50 minutes, or until deep golden brown.

MRS. NELSON LUNDBERG
Cathedral of All Saints Episcopal Church
Albany, New York

THREE CHEESE CASSEROLE *Makes 12 servings*

2 POUNDS LEAN GROUND BEEF
SALT TO TASTE
1 (14 OUNCE) JAR PIZZA SAUCE
1 (16 TO 18 OUNCE) JAR SPAGHETTI SAUCE
1 POUND SPAGHETTI (COOKED ACCORDING TO
   PACKAGE DIRECTIONS)
1 (12 OUNCE) CARTON SMALL CURD COTTAGE
   CHEESE
1 (6 TO 8 OUNCE) PACKAGE SLICED MOZZARELLA
   CHEESE
8 TO 10 OUNCES CHEDDAR CHEESE, SHREDDED

Preheat oven to 325°.

1. Grease the bottom and sides of a 9- x 13-inch pan or a large, foil pan.

2. Brown the meat in a large skillet. Add salt. Stir with a fork until the pink is gone. Drain fat.

3. Add pizza and spaghetti sauces. Place on medium heat, stirring until well mixed.

4. Place about ⅓ of the spaghetti on the bottom of the pan. Cover with cottage cheese and ⅓ of the meat sauce.

5. Add a second layer of spaghetti. Cover with mozzarella slices and ⅓ of the meat sauce.

6. Add the remaining spaghetti, the remaining meat sauce, and cover with the shredded Cheddar cheese.

7. Bake for 30 minutes.

LOIS J. MARTIN
Let Us Thank Him for Our Food
Shiloh Terrace Baptist Church
Dallas, Texas

SOUR CREAM CHICKEN ENCHILADAS *Makes 6 servings*

1 SMALL CHICKEN, COOKED AND DEBONED
1 ½ CUPS CHEDDAR CHEESE, GRATED
1 LARGE ONION, CHOPPED
1 DOZEN SMALL CORN TORTILLAS
1 ½ CUPS CHICKEN STOCK, HOT
¼ CUP (½ STICK) MARGARINE
¼ CUP ALL-PURPOSE FLOUR
1 CUP SOUR CREAM
1 SMALL CAN GREEN CHILIES
1 CUP MONTEREY JACK CHEESE, SHREDDED

1. Boil and strip meat from chicken. Chop into small pieces. Preheat oven to 350°.

2. Add cheddar cheese and onion to chicken. Stir to combine.

3. Dip tortillas in hot chicken stock to soften.

4. Place a heaping tablespoonful of chicken mixture in each tortilla. Roll and place in the casserole dish.

5. Melt margarine and blend in flour. Add chicken broth and boil until thick. Remove from heat.

6. Add sour cream and chilies to chicken broth mixture. Pour over enchiladas.

7. Bake for 30 minutes. Sprinkle with Monterey Jack cheese.

KAREN MCCARTER
Let Us Thank Him for Our Food
Shiloh Terrace Baptist Church
Dallas, Texas

SMALL TALK

The only thing more universal than green bean casserole at a covered dish gathering is gossip. As one mouth of the South puts it, "I don't like to repeat gossip, so listen carefully." Another oft-repeated phrase at a potluck is, "If you don't have anything nice to say about people, come sit by me." My problem is not with the gossip but with the people who refuse to admit that is what they're doing. You may have heard their excuses in one form or another: "I'm not gossiping; I'm simply stating facts" or "I'm sure that so-and-so would want us to pray for her because of . . ." or "I'm simply setting the story straight."

Whatever the reason, most people find it nearly impossible to resist repeating that juicy tidbit that exposes the foibles of their fellow man. At the Second Christian Church, Brother Earl decided that the gossiping was out of hand and needed to be reined in. Although he had preached many a sermon on curbing the tongue, the idle chatter increased. Finally he felt compelled to devise a plan to remind the flock in a dramatic way just how wrong it was to spread rumors. He put his plan into action at Wednesday night supper. Joyce Lynn Barker was given the first piece of bait.

"Evening, Mrs. Barker," the pastor casually remarked as he passed Joyce Lynn in the hall.

"Well, Hi-dee, Brother Earl. How is every little thing?" Joyce asked enthusiastically, hoping for some bit of news about an ailing member or a prospective visitor.

"Oh, everything's fine, I suppose . . . except for . . . Well, I don't want to burden you," he trailed off.

"No, no!" Joyce Lynn practically hyperventilated. "I would be happy to listen to any problem you need to talk about."

"Are you sure you don't mind?" Brother Earl asked.

"No, not at all. I've got all the time in the world. You just sit right down over here and share your burdens with me." Joyce Lynn purred sweetly as she contemplated just what this could be all about.

"I must tell you this is strictly confidential, and I must ask you not to repeat it to another soul," he said as she nodded emphatically and assured him of her absolute trustworthiness.

"I'm afraid that I've been spending too much time with Molly, and my wife is getting jealous." *Oh, good heavens,* Joyce Lynn thought to herself, *this is big, this is really big!*

The pastor continued. "It's just that we enjoy so many of the same things—things that my wife has no interest in. Molly is so enthusiastic, always ready for a romp."

Joyce Lynn nearly went into convulsions at this revelation. "I've got to run, Pastor. Uh, uh, my cake is melting in the car," she said rapidly as she thought, *Just wait until I tell his wife and the rest of the ladies about this!*

"You will keep this under your hat," Earl whispered.

"Oh my, yes. Don't worry about that," Joyce Lynn said as she backed away and began scanning the crowd for Earl's wife, Louella.

As she maneuvered through the crowd, Joyce stopped several ladies dead in their tracks with an urgently whispered, "Can't talk now, but it looks like the pastor is having an affair with someone named Molly! I'll get back with you when I've got more details." Well, of course, the ladies needed more than that to go on, so they followed Joyce as she made her way to Louella's side.

"Louella, you poor baby. I just heard about Molly. How bad is it?" Joyce Lynn said as six women standing behind her strained to hear.

"Well, it's gotten pretty bad. You know they are just inseparable; she's even sleeping with him now."

"Oh, my word! How do you know they're sleeping together?" Joyce Lynn gasped.

"They're right there in my bed. How could I miss it?" Louella asked with a slightly puzzled look at Joy's seemingly horrified expression.

"You're letting them sleep together in your bed?" Joyce Lynn asked incredulously. "Have you lost your mind?" she exclaimed, as the six ladies in waiting nearly fell over from trying to lean in closer.

"Well, I know some people don't like dogs in their beds, but I don't think I have lost my mind, Joyce Lynn!" Louella retorted loudly as the women gathered began to giggle.

Joyce Lynn turned bright red as she realized the blunder she had made and quickly made her way out of the room, leaving a trail of laughter behind.

The gossip mill slowed down considerably after that supper. Brother Earl mentions his dog, Molly, in his sermons from time to time and it never ceases to have a quieting effect on the congregation.

VEGETABLES

CALICO BEANS   *Makes 20 to 25 servings*

1 POUND BACON
2 POUNDS GROUND BEEF
1 LARGE ONION, CHOPPED
1 (16 OUNCE) CAN LIMA BEANS
1 (16 OUNCE) CAN PORK AND BEANS
1 (16 OUNCE) CAN KIDNEY BEANS
1 (16 OUNCE) CAN GREAT NORTHERN BEANS
1 (16 OUNCE) CAN BUTTER BEANS
1 CUP BROWN SUGAR, FIRMLY PACKED
1 (14 OUNCE) BOTTLE KETCHUP
1 TABLESPOON PREPARED MUSTARD
1 TABLESPOON VINEGAR

Preheat oven 350°.

1. Reserve 3 or 4 slices of bacon. Cook remaining bacon. Drain.

2. Brown ground beef and onion. Drain well.

3. Mix all beans (undrained) with the brown sugar, ketchup, mustard, and vinegar.

4. Crumble cooked bacon and stir into beans. In a large casserole dish, combine the beans and ground beef mixture. Mix well.

5. Spread the uncooked bacon over the top of the beans.

6. Bake for 1 hour.

BONITA GARRETT
First United Methodist Church
Edmond, Oklahoma

CARROT CASSEROLE   *Makes 6 to 8 servings*

3 CUPS CARROTS, SLICED
¾ CUP BREAD CRUMBS
2 TABLESPOONS BUTTER
2 TEASPOONS ONION, MINCED
1 TABLESPOON SUGAR

$^{1}/_{4}$ CUP THICK CREAM OR EVAPORATED MILK
$^{1}/_{2}$ CUP CHEDDAR CHEESE, GRATED

Preheat oven to 350°.

1. Place sliced carrots in saucepan that has been filled with salted water. Boil until tender. Drain water.

2. Pour carrots into a medium casserole dish. Mix in remaining ingredients, except cheese. Stir to combine.

3. Sprinkle carrot mixture with cheese.

4. Bake for 30 minutes.

JEAN ATKINSON
Banner United Methodist Church
Gothenburg, Nebraska

SPECTACULAR
SQUASH   *Makes 8 servings*

1 (8 OUNCE) PACKAGE HERB STUFFING MIX
1 STICK BUTTER OR MARGARINE, MELTED
2 POUNDS YELLOW CROOKNECK SQUASH, SLICED
$^{1}/_{2}$ LARGE ONION, SLICED
1 (10$^{3}/_{4}$ OUNCE) CAN CREAM OF CHICKEN SOUP
  (DON'T ADD MILK)
1 CUP SOUR CREAM
1 CUP CARROTS, GRATED
SALT AND PEPPER TO TASTE

Preheat oven to 350°.

1. Combine the stuffing mix with melted butter. Stir until well blended. Set aside.

2. Lightly steam squash and onion until barely cooked. Drain thoroughly.

3. Combine soup, sour cream, and grated carrots. Season with salt and pepper to taste.

4. Fold in cooked squash and onions.

5. Press half the stuffing mix into a 9- x 13-inch or 3-quart casserole dish.

6. Gently spoon squash mixture over stuffing mix in casserole. Top with remaining stuffing mix.

7. Bake for 30 minutes or until stuffing begins to brown and bubble at edges.

BOBBIE HAMMETT
Shiloh Terrace Baptist Church
Dallas, Texas

BRUSSELS SPROUTS WITH MAPLE-WALNUT VINAIGRETTE *Makes 6 servings*

4 CUPS BRUSSELS SPROUTS
4 TABLESPOONS SHERRY VINEGAR
4 TABLESPOONS PURE MAPLE SYRUP
1 TABLESPOON DIJON-STYLE MUSTARD
$\frac{1}{2}$ CUP WALNUT OIL
PINCH OF FRESHLY GRATED NUTMEG
SALT AND PEPPER
1 CUP WALNUTS, COARSELY CHOPPED

1. Steam brussels sprouts to desired tenderness.

2. Meanwhile, whisk together vinegar, maple syrup, and mustard. Gradually add in oil.

3. Season with nutmeg, salt, and pepper to taste.

4. Toss sprouts with vinaigrette dressing and walnuts. Serve immediately.

CYNTHIA NEALE
Inspiring Recipes
First Baptist Church
Macedon, New York

EGGPLANT CASSEROLE ITALIAN STYLE *Makes 4 servings*

1 (16 OUNCE) CAN TOMATO PUREE
2 (6 OUNCE) CANS TOMATO PASTE
2/3 CUP PARMESAN CHEESE, GRATED
1 MEDIUM ONION, CHOPPED
2 CLOVES GARLIC, CHOPPED
SALT TO TASTE
1 MEDIUM EGGPLANT
3/4 CUP MILK
1 EGG
1 CUP ALL-PURPOSE FLOUR
1/4 CUP VEGETABLE OIL (MORE IF NEEDED)
1 CUP PARSLEY SPRIGS
8 OUNCES MOZZARELLA CHEESE, CUT IN STRIPS
ADDITIONAL PARMESAN CHEESE

1. Mix puree, tomato paste, cheese, onion, garlic, and salt in a large saucepan. Heat to boiling. Simmer for 1 hour, stirring occasionally.

2. Peel eggplant and slice into thin strips.

3. Beat milk and egg together. Dip eggplant into the mixture.

4. Roll the strips in flour. Fry in hot oil until browned. Preheat oven to 350°.

5. In a 9- x 13-inch casserole dish, alternate the layers of eggplant, tomato sauce, parsley sprigs, and strips of mozzarella cheese.

6. Top with a sprinkling of Parmesan cheese. Bake until bubbly.

SHARON CASEY
Rose of Sharon Family Cookbook
Cottage Grove, Minnesota

GERMAN POTATO SALAD *Makes 6 servings*

6 SLICES BACON, DICED
2 TABLESPOONS ALL-PURPOSE FLOUR
1/3 CUP SUGAR
2 TEASPOONS SALT
1/8 TEASPOON BLACK PEPPER
1 EGG, SLIGHTLY BEATEN
1/4 CUP VINEGAR
1/4 CUP WATER
1/4 CUP LEMON JUICE
2 POUNDS COOKED POTATOES, PEELED, SLICED,
   AND WARM
1/2 CUP ONION, SLICED
1 TEASPOON CELERY SEED
1/4 CUP FRESH PARSLEY, MINCED AND DIVIDED

1. Brown bacon in a medium saucepan.

2. Remove bacon to drain on paper towels.

3. To drippings add flour, sugar, salt, and pepper. Cook until bubbly, stirring constantly.

4. Mix together egg, vinegar, water, and lemon juice.

5. Gradually stir egg mixture into flour mixture.

6. Cook, stirring constantly, until thick.

7. Reduce heat to low. Cook for 10 minutes.

8. Add bacon and all remaining ingredients except 2 tablespoons parsley.

9. Toss lightly.

10. Top with remaining parsley. Serve warm.

DOLORES GULAN
A Book of Favorite Recipes
Catholic Church of St. Walter
Roselle, Illinois

CHILI CORN CASSEROLE *Makes 8 servings*

1 (16 OUNCE) CAN CREAM STYLE CORN
1 (16 OUNCE) CAN WHOLE KERNEL CORN
1 CUP BISQUICK
2 EGGS
¾ CUP MILK
1 CUP CHEDDAR CHEESE, GRATED
1 (3 OUNCE) CAN GREEN CHILIES
1 TEASPOON BAKING POWDER
½ CUP VEGETABLE OIL
ADDITIONAL CHEDDAR CHEESE

Preheat oven to 350°.

1. Mix all ingredients together and pour into a greased 9- x 13-inch baking dish.

2. Sprinkle additional cheese on top.

3. Bake for 35 to 40 minutes or until set.

AVA SEALE
Justified Temptations
Richardson Heights Baptist Church
Richardson, Texas

BAKED LENTILS *Makes 4 to 6 servings*

1 ¾ CUPS LENTILS, RINSED AND DRAINED
2 CUPS WATER
2 TEASPOONS GARLIC SALT
½ TEASPOON BLACK PEPPER
¾ TEASPOON POULTRY SEASONING
2 LARGE ONIONS, CHOPPED
1 (16 OUNCE) CAN TOMATOES
2 LARGE CARROTS, SLICED
1 BAY LEAF

Preheat oven to 375°.

1. Combine all ingredients in a medium-size casserole dish.

2. Cover and bake for 1 hour or until the vegetables are tender. (Remove bay leaves.)

JEAN KRELIC
Rose of Sharon Family Cookbook
Rose of Sharon Lutheran Church
Cottage Grove, Minnesota

POTATO CROQUETTES *Makes 12 servings*

2 EGGS, SEPARATED
2 CUPS MASHED POTATOES
1 TEASPOON ONION JUICE
1 TEASPOON SALT
1 TEASPOON DRIED PARSLEY
2 TEASPOONS SOUR CREAM
DASH OF NUTMEG
1 TABLESPOON BUTTER
DASH OF CAYENNE PEPPER
1 CUP BREAD CRUMBS

Preheat oven to 375°.

1. Beat egg yolks until light. Add potatoes.

2. Add the remaining ingredients (except egg whites and bread crumbs). Pour into a medium saucepan. Stir over medium heat until thoroughly combined.

3. Remove from stove and cool.

4. In a separate bowl, beat egg whites until frothy.

5. Using a large spoon, spoon out the potato mixture, dip each spoonful in the egg whites and then into the bread crumbs.

6. Place potato croquettes on a cookie sheet that has been sprayed with cooking spray. Bake until the outside is browned and the croquettes are warmed through.

MRS. L.Y. FOOTE
Lydian Cookbook
Main Street Methodist Church
Hattiesburg, Mississippi

SWEET AND SOUR
GREEN BEANS *Makes 8 servings*

1 ONION, CHOPPED
2 CUPS GREEN BEANS, COOKED
3 TABLESPOONS BROWN SUGAR
4 TABLESPOONS VINEGAR
4 SLICES BACON, COOKED UNTIL CRISP

1. Add raw onion to hot, cooked beans.

2. Heat brown sugar and vinegar in bacon drippings. Pour over green bean mixture.

3. When ready to serve, crumble bacon on the top.

CINDY RICE
Centennial Cookbook
First Baptist Church
Laurel, Mississippi

CELERY-CHESTNUT CASSEROLE   *Makes 6 servings*

2 CUPS CELERY, DICED
SALT TO TASTE
1 (6 OUNCE) CAN WATER CHESTNUTS
1 (10¾ OUNCE) CAN CREAM OF CHICKEN SOUP
½ CUP (1 STICK) BUTTER
1 PACKAGE (34) RITZ CRACKERS, BROKEN
½ CUP SLIVERED ALMONDS

Preheat oven to 325°.

1. Place celery in a saucepan. Cover with water and add salt. Cook for 7 minutes and drain.

2. In an 8- x 8-inch casserole dish, mix the celery with the water chestnuts and soup.

3. Place the butter in a skillet and sauté the crackers and almonds until lightly browned.

4. Sprinkle the cracker mixture over the celery and water chestnut mixture.

5. Bake for 25 to 30 minutes.

CLOVER PINKERTON
Our Favorite Recipes
St. Joseph Church
Marion, Illinois

SWEETIE-PIE PEACHES   *Makes 6 servings*

1 (16 OUNCE) CAN SWEET POTATOES, HOT AND MASHED
¼ TO ½ CUP SUGAR
¼ CUP (½ STICK) MARGARINE
1 EGG

1 (13 OUNCE) CAN CARNATION EVAPORATED MILK
1 TEASPOON VANILLA EXTRACT
2 LARGE CANS PEACH HALVES, DRAINED
NUTMEG

TOPPING:
1/2 CUP BROWN SUGAR, FIRMLY PACKED
2 TABLESPOONS ALL-PURPOSE FLOUR
3 TABLESPOONS BUTTER, MELTED
1/2 CUP PECANS, CHOPPED

1. Mix first 6 ingredients and pour into a buttered casserole dish. Microwave on high for 4 to 5 minutes, or boil on the stove, stirring constantly.

2. Arrange peaches cut-side up in baking dish and sprinkle with nutmeg. Spoon sweet potato mixture into each peach half.

3. Combine topping ingredients. Mix well.

4. Cover peaches with topping. Broil 3 to 4 minutes.

BEV MARSHALL
Favorite Recipes from Our Best Cooks
Christian Bible Church
Springfield, Illinois

TATER TOTS CASEROLE   *Makes 4 to 6 servings*

        1 POUND LEAN GROUND BEEF
        1 MEDIUM ONION, CHOPPED
        1 (15 OUNCE) BAG TATER TOTS
        1 (10¾ OUNCE) CAN CREAM OF POTATO SOUP
        1 TEASPOON PAPRIKA

Preheat oven to 375°.

1. Spray a 9- x 13-inch baking pan with cooking spray.

2. Press ground beef on bottom of the casserole.

3. Layer with onion and Tater Tots.

4. Spoon the soup over the layers.

5. Sprinkle top with paprika.

6. Bake for 1 hour.

    GERT VAN VORST
    Bread of Life
    Free Will Baptist Church
    Pittsburg, Illinois

CASHEW ORANGE SUGAR SNAP PEAS   *Makes 6 servings*

        1 (16 OUNCE) PACKAGE FROZEN SUGAR SNAP PEAS
        ⅓ CUP ORANGE JUICE
        1 TABLESPOON HONEY
        1 TEASPOON CORNSTARCH
        ½ TEASPOON SALT
        ½ TEASPOON ORANGE PEEL, GRATED
        ¼ CUP CASHEWS

1. Cook peas to desired doneness as directed on package.

2. In a small saucepan mix orange juice, honey, cornstarch, and salt until well blended.

3. Cook over medium heat until mixture boils and thickens, stirring constantly.

4. Stir orange peel and cashews gently into the peas.

FAY BROWN
First Baptist Church
Angleton, Texas

TOMATO PUDDING *Makes 6 servings*

1 (20 OUNCE) CAN TOMATOES
1 CUP BROWN SUGAR, FIRMLY PACKED
$1/2$ TEASPOON SALT
$3/4$ CUP BOILING WATER
3 CUPS WHOLE-WHEAT BREAD CUBES
$1/2$ CUP (1 STICK) BUTTER, MELTED

Preheat oven to 375°.

1. Strain tomatoes through a sieve to make a pulp.

2. Add sugar and salt.

3. Stir in boiling water. Simmer for 5 minutes.

4. Place the bread cubes in a deep-dish casserole. Pour melted butter over them.

5. Stir in the boiling tomato mixture.

6. Bake for 50 minutes.

JAN ROSCHE
First Baptist Church
Angleton, Texas

READY TO RUMBLE

T he pièce de résistance of a covered dish is the decadent dessert. Scrumptious layer cakes, mile-high meringues on pies, fresh fruit cobblers, gooey fudge brownies—you name it: if it's got sugar in it, you'll probably find it on a table at the end of the line.

Going on the theory that a little competition never hurt anyone, our church decided that a bake-off would put some zing in our monthly covered dish suppers. Who could know that beneath those sweet, sensible-shoe-wearing demeanors lay the fiercely competitive spirits of Indy 500 race car drivers?

The judging was to be held in the fellowship hall an hour before the supper was to begin. Twenty-five church ladies stood behind long, dessert-laden tables, beaming at the judges, each confident that her creation was far and away the best dessert in the room. Some even wore special outfits to complement their dishes. Novis Newton wore a yellow straw hat with cherries around the brim for her Berry Cherry Cheesecake; Opal Collerd donned a hot pink apron with two embroidered pineapples that matched her Pink Pineapple Surprise Cake; and, perhaps outdoing them all, Willie Lou Dobson sported a Hawaiian mumu complete with hibiscus flowers behind her ear to coordinate with her Hawaiian Delight Soufflé.

Right before the panel of distinguished judges were about to sample their fourth coconut cream pie, there was an outcry from Willie Lou. It seemed her soufflé had collapsed as flat as a beehive hairdo in a West Texas dust storm, and she was blaming Mary Tinkle Bell. "I carried this soufflé on my granny's crocheted pillow the whole way from Talco, scarcely breathing the last five miles, and I walked in here with nary a crack. Now you have gone and sneezed *on purpose*, right over my beautiful Hawaiian Delight. I knew you were desperate to win, but I didn't think you would wipe out the competition with your nose!" Willie Lou said spitefully. Mary Tinkle retorted, "You ought to be thankful that I saved you the embarrassment of having the judges taste that thing. It's about as light as Mary Duane's pound cake, and it fell long before I sneezed!"

Now Mary Duane was insulted. "Are you calling my cake heavy? People beg me for my Sour Cream Chocolate Swirl Hazelnut Pound Cake recipe. And at least we know I didn't buy it at the store," she said, casting a suspicious eye towards the perfect loaf of pound cake in front of Viola Goodroe.

"Viola, everyone knows that's a Sara Lee pound cake you've been passing off as yours since I've known you. And just because you're the mayor's wife, nobody has ever said a word. Why, there's ten of those tin boxes in the back-seat of that tacky pink Cadillac you bought used from the Mary Kay lady," Mary Jane spewed out.

Viola was so taken aback that she staggered backwards and tripped over her sunshine yellow chiffon scarf. As she flailed wildly, trying to recover her balance, she grabbed the edge of the table, upsetting it and bringing five congealed salad rings crashing down on her head. Her wiglet dislocated from her head and, Jell-O dripping down her face, she sat in a daze amid gasps of horror heard around the room. After a moment, Viola began to smile. Standing up, she chose a cherry coke salad with Bing cherries from her lap and heaved it directly at Mary Duane. Mary Duane screamed and chunked a large piece at Mary Tinkle. Before you knew it, desserts were flying everywhere. There was a full-scale food fight happening right there in Fellowship Hall, and everyone was having the time of her life.

By the time the rest of the folks got there for the supper, the floor was covered in whipped cream and chocolate sauce. The ladies were all sitting in a heap crying because they had been laughing so hard, and the honorable judges were hiding in the men's room. No one explained a thing. They stood up, locked arms, and marched out of the room, friends forever and all forgiven.

DESSERTS

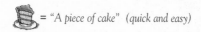 = *"A piece of cake"* *(quick and easy)*

RHUBARB
SPOON CAKE   *Makes 8 to 10 servings*

1 (18½ OUNCE) PACKAGE YELLOW OR WHITE
   CAKE MIX
4 CUPS FRESH RHUBARB, DICED
⅓ CUP ORANGE JUICE OR PINEAPPLE JUICE
1 CUP SUGAR
½ TEASPOON ORANGE PEEL, GRATED
1 TABLESPOON BUTTER

1. Prepare cake batter as directed on box.

2. Pour evenly into a 9- x 13-inch cake pan. Preheat oven to 350°.

3. Combine rhubarb, fruit juice, and sugar in heavy saucepan.

4. Cover. Cook slowly until rhubarb is nearly tender (about 10 minutes).

5. Stir in orange peel and butter.

6. Pour hot rhubarb mixture over the cake batter.

7. Bake 35 minutes or until cake is done and skewer inserted in center comes out clean.

MARY VOIGT
First Baptist Church
Avon, South Dakota

LEMON DESSERT *Makes 8 servings*

1 (14 OUNCE) CAN SWEETENED CONDENSED MILK
1 (6 OUNCE) CAN FROZEN LEMONADE, THAWED
1 (8 OUNCE) CONTAINER COOL WHIP
1 PREPARED (9-INCH) GRAHAM CRACKER CRUST
1½ CUPS FRESH STRAWBERRIES, WASHED, HULLED,
  AND SLICED

1. Combine first 3 ingredients in a large bowl. Mix until smooth.

2. Pour into prepared graham cracker crust.

3. Top with fresh strawberries. Chill for 3 hours.

MARSHA BUCHHOLZ
First Baptist Church
Avon, South Dakota

BLUE RIBBON BROWNIES *Makes 12 servings*

1 CUP ALL-PURPOSE FLOUR
1 CUP CONFECTIONERS' SUGAR
¼ CUP PLUS ½ TABLESPOON UNSWEETENED
  COCOA POWDER
¾ TEASPOON BAKING POWDER
1½ OUNCES SEMI-SWEET BAKING CHOCOLATE,
  CHOPPED
3 TABLESPOONS BUTTER
½ CUP BROWN SUGAR, FIRMLY PACKED
2 TABLESPOONS LIGHT CORN SYRUP
1 TABLESPOON WATER
2 TEASPOONS VANILLA EXTRACT
2 LARGE EGG WHITES

Preheat oven to 350°.

1. Spray an 8-inch square baking pan with cooking spray.

2. Sift first four ingredients together. Set aside.

3. Combine chocolate and butter in a saucepan over the lowest heat, stirring frequently just until melted and smooth.

4. Remove from heat and stir in brown sugar, corn syrup, water, and vanilla until well blended.

5. Beat egg whites into chocolate mixture until well blended and smooth.

6. Pour batter evenly into prepared pan.

7. Bake on the middle rack for 24 to 28 minutes or until center is almost firm.

BETH INGRAM
Taste and See That the Lord is Good
Great Hills Retreat Ministry
Austin, Texas

CHRISTMAS STRAWBERRIES *Makes 1 dozen*

2 (3 OUNCE) PACKAGES STRAWBERRY JELL-O
1 CUP PECANS, CHOPPED
¾ CUP SWEETENED CONDENSED MILK
1 CUP COCONUT
⅛ TEASPOON SALT
RED SUGAR
GREEN SUGAR
SLIVERED ALMONDS
GREEN FOOD COLORING

1. Combine first 5 ingredients. Place in refrigerator for 2 hours.

2. Shape into mock strawberries.

3. Dip bottom part in red sugar and top part in green sugar.

4. Color slivered almonds in green food coloring. When dry, insert into strawberry for stem.

NOONIE YARBROUGH
Taste and See That the Lord is Good
Great Hills Retreat Ministry
Austin, Texas

STRAWBERRY CREAM CHEESE CAKE *Makes 12 servings*

25 GRAHAM CRACKERS
1 STICK BUTTER, MELTED
2 TABLESPOONS CONFECTIONERS' SUGAR
1 (16 OUNCE) PACKAGE FROZEN STRAWBERRIES, THAWED
1 (6 OUNCE) BOX STRAWBERRY JELL-O
1 (8 OUNCE) PACKAGE CREAM CHEESE
1 CUP SUGAR
1 TEASPOON VANILLA EXTRACT
1 PINT WHIPPING CREAM

1. Prepare crust by combining crushed graham crackers, melted butter, and confectioners' sugar. Pat into a 9- x 13-inch ungreased pan. Place in refrigerator to chill.

2. Reserve the juice from the thawed strawberries. Add enough water to the juice to make 1 cup.

3. Bring juice to a boil and dissolve Jell-O in mixture. Set aside to cool, but not set.

4. In a separate bowl, combine cream cheese, sugar, and vanilla. Cream until smooth.

5. Combine cream cheese mixture with the Jell-O mixture.

6. Whip the whipping cream until thick. Fold into cream cheese and Jell-O mixture.

7. Pour mixture into graham cracker crust. Top with strawberries.

8. Chill overnight. Cut into squares to serve.

DEBBIE WAYE
Our Favorite Recipes
Heritage Presbyterian Church
Oklahoma City, Oklahoma

CHOCOLATE PIZZA *Makes 8 servings*

PARCHMENT PAPER
1 ½ CUPS SEMI-SWEET CHOCOLATE CHIPS
1 CUP BUTTERSCOTCH CHIPS
¾ CUP MINIATURE MARSHMALLOWS
¾ CUP DRY ROASTED PEANUTS, CHOPPED
¾ CUP CRUSHED RIPPLED POTATO CHIPS
2 TABLESPOONS FLAKED COCONUT
¼ CUP PLAIN CHOCOLATE CANDIES (SUCH AS M&Ms)
4 OUNCES WHITE CHOCOLATE, BROKEN INTO SQUARES
1 TEASPOON SOLID SHORTENING

1. Draw one 10-inch circle on parchment paper. Place on a baking sheet and set aside.

2. In a medium-size mixing bowl, combine chocolate and butterscotch chips. Microwave at 50 percent power for 4 to 6 minutes, stirring once or until the chocolate melts and can be stirred smooth.

3. Stir in marshmallows, peanuts, and potato chips. Mix well to coat.

4. Spread mixture evenly to cover the 10-inch circle.

5. Sprinkle with coconut.

6. Top pizza with chocolate candies. Set aside.

7. In a 2-cup measure, combine white chocolate and shortening. Microwave for 3 to 4 minutes or until melted, stirring once.

8. Drizzle the chocolate over the pizza. Chill until firm (about 2 hours).

9. Peel off the parchment paper and place on a serving plate.

CAROLYN SCOTT
Mira Mesa Presbyterian Church
Mira Mesa, California

CHOCOLATE
ZUCCHINI CAKE   *Makes 12 servings*

$\frac{1}{2}$ CUP (1 STICK) MARGARINE, SOFTENED TO ROOM
   TEMPERATURE
$\frac{1}{2}$ CUP VEGETABLE OIL
1 $\frac{3}{4}$ CUPS SUGAR
2 EGGS, WELL BEATEN
1 TEASPOON VANILLA EXTRACT
2 $\frac{1}{2}$ CUPS ALL-PURPOSE FLOUR
$\frac{1}{2}$ TEASPOON BAKING POWDER
1 TEASPOON BAKING SODA
$\frac{1}{2}$ TEASPOON GROUND CLOVES
$\frac{1}{2}$ TEASPOON CINNAMON
4 TEASPOONS COCOA
$\frac{1}{2}$ CUP BUTTERMILK
2 CUPS ZUCCHINI, GRATED
$\frac{1}{2}$ CUP SEMI-SWEET CHOCOLATE CHIPS
ICING (SEE FOLLOWING RECIPE)

Preheat oven to 350°.

1. Cream together the margarine, oil, sugar, eggs, and vanilla. Set aside.

2. Sift together the flour, baking powder, soda, cloves, cinnamon, and cocoa.

3. Sift and add to creamed mixture alternately with buttermilk.

4. Add zucchini and mix well.

5. Pour half the batter into a bundt pan. Sprinkle with ¼ cup of the chocolate chips.

6. Pour rest of batter into pan. Sprinkle with remaining chocolate chips.

7. Bake for 40 to 50 minutes or until a skewer inserted in center comes out clean. When cool, top with Favorite Chocolate Icing (see following recipe).

FRANCES THOMAS
Favorite Hometown Recipes
Cumberland Presbyterian Church
Norris City, Illinois

FAVORITE CHOCOLATE ICING

2 CUPS SUGAR
1 STICK BUTTER
$\frac{1}{2}$ CUP EVAPORATED MILK
2 TABLESPOONS COCOA POWDER
1 TEASPOON VANILLA EXTRACT

1. In a heavy saucepan, combine all ingredients, except the vanilla. Bring to a boil.

2. Using an electric mixer, beat the icing for 2 minutes.

3. Remove from heat and add vanilla. Continue beating until the icing begins to thicken.

4. Pour icing over the cooled cake.

RASPBERRY PIE *Makes 8 servings*

2 CUPS FROZEN RASPBERRIES
$\frac{1}{4}$ CUP COLD WATER
2 TABLESPOONS BUTTER
$\frac{1}{2}$ CUP SUGAR
1 TEASPOON LEMON JUICE
PINCH OF SALT
3 TABLESPOONS CORNSTARCH
$\frac{1}{4}$ CUP COLD WATER
1 (9-INCH) BAKED CHOCOLATE PIE CRUST
   (SEE FOLLOWING RECIPE)
WHIPPED CREAM

1. Defrost, drain, and reserve juice from raspberries.

2. In a small saucepan combine raspberry juice, $\frac{1}{4}$ cup water, butter, sugar, lemon juice, and salt. Place over medium heat, stir constantly until thickened.

3. Dissolve cornstarch in remaining $\frac{1}{4}$ cup cold water.

4. Add cornstarch mixture to the cooked liquids, stirring constantly until thickened.

5. Stir in the berries. Pour into a pie crust.

6. Chill until set. Serve with fresh whipped cream and additional berries, if desired.

DONNA PETERS
Family Favorites
Mira Mesa Presbyterian Church
Mira Mesa, California

CHOCOLATE
PIE CRUST *Makes 2 (8-inch) pie crusts*

1 ¾ CUPS ALL-PURPOSE FLOUR
¼ CUP COCOA POWDER
1 CUP SOLID SHORTENING
PINCH OF SALT
1 TEASPOON SUGAR
1 EGG
1 TABLESPOON VINEGAR
7 TABLESPOONS WATER

Preheat oven to 400°.

1. Sift together flour and cocoa.

2. Cut in the shortening, salt, and sugar.

3. Beat in egg.

4. Add vinegar and water.

5. Mix until it holds together enough to roll out.

6. Roll crust to a ¼-inch thickness. Place into pie pan to bake.

7. Bake for 15 minutes.

LEROY'S
ENGLISH TRIFLE *Makes 10 to 12 servings*

1 ANGEL FOOD CAKE, THINLY SLICED WITH THE
  BROWN TRIMMED OFF
STRAWBERRY PRESERVES
1 (6 OUNCE) PACKAGE STRAWBERRY JELL-O
1 (16 OUNCE) PACKAGE FROZEN STRAWBERRIES,
  THAWED AND DIVIDED
4 BANANAS, SLICED (PLACE IN SMALL AMOUNT OF
  LEMON JUICE TO PREVENT BROWNING)
1 (6 OUNCE) PACKAGE VANILLA PUDDING MIX
  (NOT INSTANT)
1/2 PINT WHIPPING CREAM, WHIPPED
PECANS, FINELY CHOPPED

1. Spread one layer of angel food cake slices with the strawberry preserves. Make this the bottom layer in a large crystal bowl.

2. Prepare and pour the hot Jell-O over the cake layer. Top with about 1/2 cup of the strawberries.

3. Place a layer of the sliced bananas on the strawberry layer.

4. Repeat layering 3 times.

5. Place in the refrigerator until firm.

6. Prepare pudding according to the package directions. As soon as pudding has thickened, pour over the trifle layers.

7. Spread the whipped cream over the pudding layer, then sprinkle with pecans.

8. Refrigerate at least 12 hours before serving.

LEROY TILL
Christmas with the Tills
First Baptist Church
Dallas, Texas

PEACH ICE CREAM *Makes 1 quart*

6 RIPE PEACHES
2 CUPS SUGAR, DIVIDED
1 TEASPOON LEMON JUICE
1 CUP MILK
2 (14 1/4 OUNCE) CANS EVAPORATED MILK
6 EGGS, SLIGHTLY BEATEN
1 (14 OUNCE) CAN SWEETENED CONDENSED MILK
1 TEASPOON VANILLA EXTRACT

1. Peel peaches, and cut 4 peaches into chunks. Mix with 1/4 cup sugar.

2. Puree the other 2 peaches with the lemon juice in a blender.

3. Heat the milk and evaporated milk together.

4. Combine eggs and remaining sugar in the top of a double boiler. Slowly add milk mixture, stirring constantly.

5. Add condensed milk and peach puree.

6. Cook, whisking constantly until the mixture is thick and coats the back of a spoon. Remove from heat. Cool mixture.

7. Stir in vanilla and peach chunks. Pour into ice cream maker.

8. Freeze according to the manufacturer's instructions.

KEN BAKER
Bless the Cooks
First Church of Christ
Eldorado, Illinois

MOCHA THREE LAYER CAKE *Makes 10 servings*

⅔ CUP MARGARINE, SOFTENED TO ROOM
   TEMPERATURE
2 CUPS SUGAR
2 EGGS, BEATEN
½ CUP BUTTERMILK
1 TEASPOON BAKING SODA
4 HEAPING TABLESPOONS COCOA POWDER
2 CUPS ALL-PURPOSE FLOUR
1 CUP BOILING WATER
1 TEASPOON VANILLA EXTRACT

FILLING:
¼ CUP (½ STICK) BUTTER, SOFTENED TO ROOM
   TEMPERATURE
3 TABLESPOONS COCOA POWDER
2 TABLESPOONS STRONG COFFEE
1 POUND CONFECTIONERS' SUGAR
CREAM (IF NEEDED)

Preheat oven to 325°.

1. Cream margarine and sugar.

2. Add eggs, buttermilk, soda, cocoa, and flour. Beat well.

3. Add boiling water and vanilla. Stir until well blended.

4. Pour batter evenly into 3 (8-inch) round cake pans.

5. Bake for 20 to 25 minutes. Remove from oven and cool on wire racks.

6. For filling: cream butter and blend in remaining ingredients.

7. Add cream, if needed, to thin. Spread filling on the top and between the layers of the cooled cake.

OPLE COLLARD
Centennial Cookbook
Polytechnic United Methodist Church
Fort Worth, Texas

STRAWBERRY PECAN CAKE *Makes 10 servings*

1 (18½ OUNCE) PACKAGE WHITE CAKE MIX
1 (6 OUNCE) BOX STRAWBERRY JELL-O
¾ CUP VEGETABLE OIL
½ CUP MILK
4 EGGS, ADDED ONE AT A TIME
1 CUP FROZEN SLICED STRAWBERRIES, THAWED
1 CUP SHREDDED COCONUT
1 CUP PECANS

FROSTING:
1 STICK MARGARINE, SOFTENED TO ROOM
   TEMPERATURE
1 (1 POUND) BOX CONFECTIONERS' SUGAR
½ CUP PECANS
½ CUP COCONUT
FROZEN SLICED STRAWBERRIES, THAWED

Preheat oven to 350°.

1. Combine first 8 ingredients. Mix according to the cake mix directions.

2. Lightly spray 3 (8-inch) cake pans with cooking spray. Fill each pan evenly with batter. Bake for 20 to 25 minutes.

3. Cool on a wire rack.

4. For frosting: Mix softened margarine with sugar. Add pecans, coconut, and just enough thawed strawberries to enable you to spread on a cold cake.

SYBIL JONES
Seasoned with Love
Cornerstone Assembly of God Church
Bethany, Oklahoma

PINEAPPLE PIE *Makes 6 servings*

1 (20 OUNCE) CAN CRUSHED PINEAPPLE
2 (3½ OUNCE) BOXES SUGAR-FREE INSTANT
   VANILLA PUDDING
1 (16 OUNCE) CARTON LITE SOUR CREAM
PREPARED GRAHAM CRACKER CRUST
LITE COOL WHIP
¼ CUP CHOPPED NUTS

1. Combine first 3 ingredients. Mix well. Pour into a graham cracker crust.

2. Top with Cool Whip and sprinkle with nuts.

3. Chill until ready to serve.

JOAN MOSBY
Feeding the Flock
Jonesboro First Baptist Church
Jonesboro, Illinois

BANANA SPLIT PIE *Makes 6 to 8 servings*

1 CUP CONFECTIONERS' SUGAR
1 STICK BUTTER, SOFTENED TO ROOM TEMPERATURE
1 EGG
1 (9- OR 10-INCH) GRAHAM CRACKER CRUST
1 (6-OUNCE) CAN CRUSHED PINEAPPLE, DRAINED
2 TO 3 BANANAS
1 (8 OUNCE) CARTON WHIPPED TOPPING
CHOPPED PECANS
CHOCOLATE SYRUP
MARASCHINO CHERRIES

1. Combine the sugar, butter, and egg until very creamy. Pour into pie crust.

2. Drain the pineapple juice into a shallow bowl. Pour the crushed pineapple over the creamed mixture.

3. Slice the bananas lengthwise. Dip in the pineapple juice and place over the pineapple.

4. Cover with whipped topping. Drizzle chocolate over the topping. Sprinkle with pecans and cherries.

ANGIE ESCUE
Feeding the Flock
Friendship General Baptist Church
Energy, Illinois

BUTTERSCOTCH CAKE *Makes 10 servings*

1 (6 OUNCE) BOX BUTTERSCOTCH PUDDING
2 CUPS MILK
$1/2$ CUP VEGETABLE OIL
1 ($18 1/2$ OUNCE) PACKAGE YELLOW CAKE MIX
1 (12 OUNCE) PACKAGE BUTTERSCOTCH CHIPS
1 CUP PECANS, CHOPPED

Preheat oven to 350°.

1. Cook pudding with milk, according to package directions.

2. Combine pudding, oil, and cake mix. Pour into a 9- x 13-inch ungreased cake pan.

3. Pour the butterscotch chips and pecans over the top. Bake for 30 minutes. Cool and serve.

STACEY AND JOLENE VALEU
Favorite Recipes from Our Best Cooks
Christian Bible Church
Springfield, Illinois

ORANGE SLICE COOKIES *Makes 2 dozen*

FLOUR
1 POUND ORANGE SLICE CANDIES
2 CUPS ALL-PURPOSE FLOUR
2 CUPS BROWN SUGAR, FIRMLY PACKED
1 CUP NUTS, CHOPPED
4 EGGS
1 TEASPOON VANILLA EXTRACT

Preheat oven to 250°.

1. Cut each orange slice into 3 or 4 pieces. In a medium-size bowl, toss enough flour with orange slices to coat lightly.

2. Add 2 cups flour, sugar and nuts. Toss again.

3. Add eggs and vanilla. Mix well (the dough will be stiff).

4. Spread in a greased and floured 9- x 13-inch pan. Bake for 1 hour.

5. Cool and cut into squares.

BETSY FISHER
Jubilee Cookbook
Highland Park United Methodist Church
Dallas, Texas

CARROT COOKIES *Makes 3 dozen*

½ CUP (1 STICK) BUTTER, SOFTENED TO ROOM
   TEMPERATURE
½ CUP SUGAR
½ CUP BROWN SUGAR, FIRMLY PACKED
1 EGG
½ TEASPOON VANILLA EXTRACT
1 CUP ALL-PURPOSE FLOUR
½ CUP CARROTS, FINELY GRATED (DO NOT PACK
   DOWN)
½ CUP FLAKED COCONUT

1 CUP QUICK-COOKING OATS, UNCOOKED
¾ CUP WALNUTS, CHOPPED

Preheat oven to 350°.

1. Cream butter and sugars. Add egg and vanilla. Mix thoroughly.

2. Mix together flour, carrots, and coconut.

3. Add remaining ingredients. Stir to combine.

4. Drop by teaspoonfuls onto greased baking sheets.

5. Bake for 8 to 10 minutes.

PAT WATSON
Cooking with Love
Glen's Creek Baptist Church
Versailles, Kentucky

BUTTER CRISPS *Makes 3 dozen*

1¼ CUPS BUTTER, SOFTENED TO ROOM
   TEMPERATURE
1¼ CUPS CONFECTIONERS' SUGAR
3 CUPS CAKE FLOUR, DIVIDED
¼ TEASPOON SALT
1 EGG
1 CUP NUTS, CHOPPED
1 TABLESPOON VANILLA EXTRACT

1. In a large bowl, cream butter and sugar.

2. Add one cup of flour and salt.

3. Add egg and beat well.

4. Add remaining flour, nuts, and vanilla.

5. Shape into rolls and chill. Preheat oven to 375°.

6. Slice and place on cookie sheets. Bake 10 to 12 minutes.

MRS. LES MCKAY
Meals from the Manse: Favorite Recipes from the Wives of Great Preachers
Cambridge, Massachusetts

LEMON WHIPPERSNAPS *Makes 4 dozen*

1 EGG
1 (18½ OUNCE) PACKAGE LEMON CAKE MIX
2 CUPS (4½ OUNCES) COOL WHIP, THAWED
½ CUP CONFECTIONERS' SUGAR

Preheat oven to 350°.

1. Combine egg, cake mix, and Cool Whip in a large bowl. Stir until well combined.

2. Drop by teaspoonfuls into powdered sugar. Roll to coat.

3. Place 1½-inches apart onto a greased cookie sheet. Bake for 10 to 15 minutes.

DOROTHY MILLER
Moscow United Methodist Church Cookbook
Moscow United Methodist Church
Moscow, Kansas

APPLE PIE *Makes 8 servings*

4 LARGE BAKING APPLES
½ CUP SUGAR
2 TABLESPOONS ALL-PURPOSE FLOUR
½ TEASPOON NUTMEG
1 (9- OR 10-INCH) UNBAKED DEEP DISH PIE CRUST
2 TABLESPOONS LEMON JUICE

TOPPING:
½ CUP SUGAR
½ CUP ALL-PURPOSE FLOUR
½ CUP (1 STICK) BUTTER

Preheat oven to 425°.

1. Peel and cut apples into small pieces.

2. Combine sugar, flour, and nutmeg. Stir to combine.

3. Sprinkle over the apples to coat well.

4. Spoon apples into the pie shell. Drizzle with lemon juice.

5. For the topping: Combine sugar and flour. Cut in the butter to form coarse crumbs.

6. Sprinkle over the apples.

7. Place on a large cookie sheet. Bake for 1 hour.

8. Remove pie and cool on rack.

GAIL HEFTON
Justified Temptations
Richardson Heights Baptist Church
Richardson, Texas

EGG CUSTARD *Makes 4 servings*

2 CUPS WARM MILK
3 EGGS, SEPARATED
$\frac{1}{2}$ CUP SUGAR
$\frac{1}{4}$ TEASPOON SALT
1 TABLESPOON BUTTER, MELTED
$\frac{1}{4}$ TEASPOON NUTMEG
$\frac{1}{4}$ TEASPOON LEMON OR VANILLA EXTRACT

Preheat oven to 400°.

1. Combine all ingredients, except the egg whites. Beat until well combined but not foamy.

2. Beat egg whites until stiff but not dry. Fold into other mixture. Stir thoroughly to combine.

3. Pour ingredients into a 3½-cup soufflé dish. Place the soufflé dish in a 8- x 8- x 2-inch baking dish on an oven rack. Pour boiling water into the baking dish around the soufflé dish.

4. Bake for 15 minutes. Reduce the heat to 325° and bake 10 minutes longer. A knife inserted in the center that comes out clean is a good indicator of doneness.

MRS. BUFORD SELF
Centennial Cookbook
Elizabeth Baptist Church
Shelby, North Carolina

PEAR PRESERVE CAKE *Makes 10 servings*

¾ CUP BUTTER
2 CUPS SUGAR
3 EGGS
1 CUP SOFT PEAR PRESERVES, DRAINED
1 SMALL BOTTLE CHOPPED MARASCHINO CHERRIES, DRAINED
3 CUPS FLOUR
1 TEASPOON SODA
1 TEASPOON NUTMEG
1 TEASPOON CINNAMON
1 TEASPOON ALLSPICE
2 TEASPOONS BAKING POWDER
¼ TEASPOON SALT
1 CUP NUTS, CHOPPED
1 CUP BUTTERMILK
FILLING (SEE FOLLOWING RECIPE)

1. In a large mixing bowl, cream together the butter and sugar.

2. Add eggs one at a time, mixing after each addition.

3. Add pear preserves and cherries and stir to combine.

4. In a medium-sized mixing bowl, sift together all the dry ingredients (except the baking soda).

5. Dissolve the soda in the buttermilk.

6. Toss a little of the flour mixture in with the nuts to lightly coat.

7. Add the buttermilk and flour mixture alternately and mix to combine.

8. Fold in the floured nuts.

9. Grease and flour 3 (8-inch) cake pans. Evenly divide the cake batter between the 3 pans.

10. Bake at 300° for 30 to 35 minutes or until a toothpick inserted comes out clean.

PEAR PRESERVES CAKE CARAMEL FILLING

3 TABLESPOONS SUGAR
⅓ CUP EVAPORATED MILK
6 TABLESPOONS BUTTER
1 POUND BOX OF POWDERED SUGAR

1. Place sugar in a heavy skillet over medium heat to carmelize. You will need to stir this constantly.

2. Add the evaporated milk and butter to the sugar and stir.

3. Pour the ingredients into a medium bowl and add the powdered sugar and mix to combine, adding more of the evaporated milk if it is too thick.

4. Spread between the three layers as a filling. If you would like to ice the entire cake, double the caramel filling.

GRACE PEARY JARRELL
First Baptist Church
Hattiesburg, Mississippi

COCONUT POUND CAKE *Makes 12 servings*

3 CUPS SUGAR
2 STICKS BUTTER
$\frac{1}{2}$ CUP CRISCO
6 EGGS
3 CUPS FLOUR
$\frac{1}{2}$ TEASPOON SALT
$\frac{1}{2}$ TEASPOON BAKING POWDER
1 CUP MILK
1 TABLESPOON VANILLA
1 TABLESPOON COCONUT FLAVORING

1. In a large bowl combine sugar, butter, and Crisco. Mix thoroughly to combine.

2. Add eggs one at a time, beating after each addition.

3. In a medium bowl, sift together the dry ingredients.

4. Add the flavorings to the milk.

5. Add the flour and the milk alternately, stirring to thoroughly combine.

6. Grease and flour a 10-inch tube pan. Pour butter into pan.

7. Bake at 350° for 1 hour or until a toothpick inserted comes out clean.

GERTRUDE BEAM CABANISS
First Baptist Church
Shelby, North Carolina

ANGEL DAINTIES *Makes 12–15 servings*

1 ANGEL FOOD CAKE
1 STICK BUTTER
2 CUPS SUGAR
$\frac{1}{4}$ CUP COCOA
$\frac{1}{2}$ CUP MILK
1 TEASPOON VANILLA

1. Purchase a store-bought angel food cake and tear into pieces.

2. In a medium saucepan, melt the butter over medium heat.

3. Add the remaining ingredients and bring to a boil; boil for 2 minutes while beating with a mixer.

4. Remove from heat and continue beating until chocolate sauce begins to thicken.

5. Dip the torn angel food cake pieces into the chocolate and place on wax paper to dry.

ANNIE VERNON JETER HULL
Highland Heights Baptist Church
Memphis, Tennessee

SWEETHEART
BANQUET

Nadine and Scharleanne stood talking after Monday night visitation, lamenting the fact that there hadn't been a Median Adult Sweetheart Banquet in years and how their husbands hadn't been romantic in aeons and just what were they going to do about it? They decided to speak to Louella—their pastor Brother Earl's wife—about this dismal situation and see what her opinion was. She brought in Sue Ann Peavy, the Outreach director, for a consultation, and lo and behold a party was planned for February 14.

The Fellowship Hall was transformed into a passion-pink wonderland of hearts, flowers, and candlelight. The whole menu revolved around a heart-shaped, red-ketchup-covered meatloaf; pink-frosted, heart-shaped cupcakes for dessert; and pink lemonade to drink. There were heart-shaped balloons floating above the tables and heart-shaped candies and confetti sprinkled on the tabletops. There was even an open styrofoam heart covered with pink crepe paper for the couples to stand under and have their picture made.

Everything was perfectly lovely, and the evening just dripped with romance until the men arrived. They spoiled everything! First, they made numerous references to the old Alka-Seltzer commercial about the newlywed husband who had just eaten his bride's heart-shaped meatloaf and needed an antacid. Then they took to running and leaping through the styrofoam heart like trained dogs at the circus. Finally it busted in two, right along with the women's dreams of some enchanted evening. The broken heart, along with Jimmy Lee's sprained ankle, put a damper on the men's antics, and they settled down at the tables to eat.

During the men's performances the women had huddled to come up with an appropriate punishment. They decided to announce that before one crumb was eaten, each man would have to come to the podium, speak into the microphone, and tell everyone ten reasons why he loved his wife. Under much grumbling and resistance each man got up red-faced, and gave his ten reasons, some silly and some heartrending. After the last man finished there wasn't a dry eye in the crowd.

The Sweetheart Banquet has become an annual event looked forward to like no other, and the tradition of the husbands speaking of their love for their wives has become the highlight of the evening.

BEVERAGES

 = *"A piece of cake"* *(quick and easy)*

PINE-ORANGE PUNCH
Makes 25 to 30 servings

4 (6 OUNCE) CANS FROZEN ORANGE JUICE
12 CANS WATER
2 PACKAGES ORANGE KOOL-AID
1 (46 OUNCE) CAN PINEAPPLE JUICE

Combine all ingredients and chill well.

KAY JOHNSON
Cumberland Presbyterian Church
Norris City, Illinois

HOT SPICED APRICOT TEA
Makes about 6 cups

10 WHOLE CLOVES
2 (2-INCH) STICKS CINNAMON
3 CUPS WATER
2 REGULAR-SIZE TEA BAGS
2 (12 OUNCE) CANS APRICOT NECTAR
$\frac{1}{2}$ CUP SUGAR
$\frac{1}{4}$ CUP LEMON JUICE

1. Place cloves and cinnamon in a cheesecloth bag. Set aside.

2. In a large saucepan, bring the water to a boil.

3. Add tea bags and remove from heat. Cover and steep 5 minutes.

4. Remove tea bags.

5. Add spices, apricot nectar, sugar, and lemon juice.

6. Bring to a boil.

7. Remove spices. Serve hot or cold over ice.

COOKBOOK COMMITTEE
The Jubilee of Our Many Blessings Cookbook
Highland Park United Methodist Church
Dallas, Texas

SHERBET PUNCH *Makes 15 to 18 servings*

4 PACKAGES KOOL-AID
2 QUARTS WATER
4 CUPS SUGAR
1 (46 OUNCE) CAN PINEAPPLE JUICE
1 QUART SHERBET, SOFTENED
2 (1½ LITER) BOTTLES GINGER ALE

1. Mix and refrigerate Kool-Aid, water, and sugar.

2. Add remaining ingredients, except ginger ale.

3. Stir thoroughly and chill. Add ginger ale just before serving.

GLORIA WALL
Bread of Life
Freewill Baptist Church
Pittsburg, Illinois

COFFEE PUNCH *Makes 15 to 18 servings*

¼ CUP INSTANT COFFEE
½ CUP SUGAR
2 QUARTS WATER
2 CUPS COLD MILK
2 TEASPOONS VANILLA EXTRACT
1 QUART VANILLA ICE CREAM
1 CUP WHIPPING CREAM, WHIPPED
NUTMEG

1. Combine instant coffee and sugar until well blended. Add water and stir until sugar is dissolved.

2. Stir in milk and vanilla.

3. Chill mixture thoroughly.

4. Just before serving, place partially softened ice cream into a chilled punch bowl.

5. Pour coffee mixture over ice cream.

6. Top with whipped cream. Sprinkle with nutmeg, if desired.

For mocha punch: substitute chocolate ice cream and add ½ teaspoon almond flavoring.

MILDRED MCALLISTER
Centennial Cookbook
Polytechnic United Methodist Church
Fort Worth, Texas

CRANBERRY RASPBERRY PUNCH *Makes 4½ quarts punch*

1 (12 OUNCE) FROZEN CONCENTRATE
  CRANBERRY-RASPBERRY JUICE COCKTAIL
1½ LITER BOTTLE SCHWEPPES RASPBERRY
  GINGER ALE

1. Mix juice concentrate according to can directions. (This will make 48 ounces.)

2. Add raspberry ginger ale and stir. (Depending on the size of your punch bowl, you will need 1½ to 2 bottles of ginger ale.)

*Make an ice ring using raspberries and blueberries and float in punch bowl just before serving.

GAY BOGGESS
Inspiring Recipes
First Baptist Church
Macedon, New York

PRALINE
PASSION

Everybody has a favorite dish he always looks forward to seeing in the food lineup at a covered dish. It might be Lilly Pearl's fried chicken or Miss Ida's devil's food cake; but if it's not on the table, the meal just isn't the same.

Bobby Fred Peavy had a weakness for pecan pralines. Specifically, Mrs. Beulah Burns's pralines. He just couldn't get enough of them. This was probably because his mama in her infinite wisdom only allowed him to have two after he cleaned his plate and asked nicely. Bobby Fred always thought that if he could just once eat a whole plateful of pralines, he would be happy enough to die and go to heaven.

One fine spring evening, Bobby Fred was headed to the dessert table to receive his quota of two pralines when he spied a Tupperware dish sitting on the tailgate of Mrs. Burns's station wagon. Nobody was around as he casually sauntered over to investigate. Bingo! It was the backup container of pralines. *This was too good to be true!* Destiny had led him to this moment. *No one had* to know. *Mrs. Burns would think that the pralines had been used up on the serving line and someone had brought over the reserves,* he thought to himself. Trouble was, where to store them? His mama was expecting him back in a few minutes, and his pockets were already full with his Swiss Army knife, a couple of dead frogs, and a yo-yo. He took off his cap to scratch his head when it dawned on him like a bolt of lightning: at least ten pralines would fit inside his cap, more if he crunched them up! Bobby Fred was busy stuffing his cap full when he heard the first clap of thunder.

Better get back over to Mama's table to help pick up before the storm hits, he thought to himself, as he hurried back to the family. *I'll have plenty of time to eat these awesome pralines tonight in my bed.* As the raindrops began to fall, Bobby Fred started gathering their belongings together, oblivious to the effect the rain was having on his pralines.

His little sister, Betty Fred, was the first to notice. "What's that gross brown stuff running down your face?" she asked in that loud, obnoxious manner that only younger sisters can manage. As he wiped his face to see what she meant, his mama caught a glimpse as well. "Is that tobacco juice on your face?" she demanded. Then his older brother, Billy Fred, took a swipe at his face and gave it the sniff test. "This is sugar," he crowed. "Bobby Fred is melting, 'cause he's made of sugar, like a girl!"

With a half cup full of sticky pecans on his head and brown syrup running down his back and chest, Bobby Fred gave it his best shot. "Mama, I was just trying to save the pralines from the rain by putting them under my hat." Mama gave him a long, hard suspicious look, sighed, and said, "Well, I guess if anybody was going to save the pralines, it would have to be you. Take off your hat and eat what you can, then clean off the rest."

Bobby Fred Peavy went to bed a happy boy that night, and no one was ever the wiser.

FEEDING THE
FLOCK

SETTING UP

Memories feast on large gatherings. Recollections of childhood are crowded with long, loud dinners with heaping platters of food shared with favorite friends and relatives sitting elbow to elbow, plastic fork in hand. Big family reunions, church fellowship meals, and church picnics lend themselves to some of the best eating in our country. Would you bring a bad recipe to a covered dish?

If you are planning a covered dish event, how do you make sure you don't end up with five fishes and one loaf of bread? The first step to a successful church supper, or any gathering where food is the main event, is planning. The points in this chapter are going to take you through a step-by-step process for painlessly putting a large dinner on the table.

PLANNING A LARGE EVENT

Planning and teamwork make successful covered dishes. Everything else has a committee, so why shouldn't the favorite food feast? Here is one way to look at your operation without dumping the whole bushel of potatoes on your church hostess.

1. Select five or six persons to be on the major committee; more people prolong meetings and slow decision making. However, if you are heading a committee, one the following suggestions will help the delegation process and give you some ideas for organizing your efforts.

2. Assign each person a job, e.g., lining up dessert makers, and asking people to serve.

3. Set a mutually convenient time for meetings and run them fast; volunteers often have full-time jobs as well as family responsibilities. Try early morning meetings before daily routines set in; members rarely miss.

4. Plan the menu a month or more in advance. Check supplies and any possible conflicts with the church calendar.

5. What are you trying to accomplish? Is it an after-Sunday-evening-service dessert party, a hungry man's feast, a club meeting, or a family reunion? Is the meal given in someone's honor, and, if so, will there be a receiving line, speeches, or presentations?

6. For a typical church covered dish, will foods be assigned or will people be asked to bring a dish to serve their own families, plus two or four? A "bring anything" supper could yield you twenty creamy corn casseroles, a relish tray for four, and one platter of crispy fried chicken. If that is a risk, ask all whose names begin with A to L to bring main dishes;

M to S people, salad or vegetables; and T to Z folk, desserts. The church usually provides the plates, eating utensils, napkins, and drinks.

7. A good traffic pattern for buffet service is an essential ingredient for creating an inviting atmosphere as well as seeing that everyone is served in a timely fashion. Consider how the supper will be served. Hot foods should be served hot, and cold foods should be served cold. What kind of equipment is needed to make this happen, and does the church have that equipment? A well-set buffet helps prevent traffic jams. Stack clean plates at the starter end, then the main dishes and vegetables. Gravy or drippy food should be set towards the front of the table to prevent drips as they are ladled, and sprinkle-ons (garnishes for chili, condiments, salad dressings) should be set in front of the foods they complement. Napkins and dinnerware can either be placed next to the plates on the buffet table or set on dining tables.

8. If you are feeding an extra large group, and space allows, set up more than one serving line. Make both sides of the table similar so curious tasters don't bounce from one line to another. Coffee and dessert are served most efficiently from other tables.

9. The kitchen should be supervised to keep everything organized and orderly.

10. The cleanup group may scrape dirty plates and separate used silverware and dishes. Somebody must be responsible for making sure the dinnerware is back in appropriate cupboards, and that the kitchen is left in an orderly fashion.

11. Delegation is an art of fitting the right person to a job. Men and women of varied abilities volunteer, and making that work for you establishes your team. A well-established team translates to a successful special event.

HOW MUCH IS ENOUGH?

Nothing is worse than attending a dinner, getting your turn in the buffet line, and seeing nothing but bottoms of the cleaned-out dishes. So what is a rule of thumb? The following guidelines will help you plan or prepare for parties of 10, 20 to 25, or 50.

Get out your calculator and figure how much you will need of what and plan accordingly.

Allow 1 pound of fresh vegetables with little waste (snap beans), or 2 pounds with shells or heavy trimmings (green peas), for every 3 to 4 people. A 16-ounce can or a 10-ounce package of frozen vegetables serves 3 to 4. Buy 4 ounces of lean ground beef for an average hamburger, 6 to 8 ounces for teenager size.

SERVING 10
- 3 casseroles that will serve 4 people, or one main meat that allows a 4-ounce serving per person
- 2 vegetables that will serve 6 people
- 1 or 2 desserts (most cakes will serve at least 10 people)
- 1 large loaf of bread

SERVING 25
- 5 casseroles that will serve 6 people, or two main meats with enough to serve 15 people each
- 5 vegetables that will serve 6 people
- 2 or 3 desserts
- 3 large loaves of bread

SERVING 50
- 10 casseroles that will serve 6 people, or two main meats with enough to serve 30 people each
- 12 vegetables that will serve 6 people
- 6 desserts that will serve 10 people
- 6 large loaves of bread

TABLE FOR TEN

Informal Sunday brunch is a relaxing way to transform an ordinary Sunday, whether it is pregame grub or an after church get-together. Preplanning and favorite recipes from your friends' files make Sunday afternoon a time for relaxing and enjoying the day. The hostess can prepare the dessert ahead and provide coffee, teas, and flavored waters and delegate the rest of the menu.

BRUNCH MENU

- Fresh fruits
- Croissants and fruit muffins with apple butter and homemade preserves
- Omelet buffet (need 25 eggs and 2 sticks butter; see recipe for basic omelet below)

    Ask guests to bring eggs and various ingredients and set up an omelet station just like the hotels. Ask each guest to bring 2 cups of chopped omelet fillings such as cheeses, asparagus, broccoli, carrots, bacon, spinach, and onion.
- Baked peaches with nutmeg butter
- Favorite dessert

OMELET

2 EGGS
1 TABLESPOON WATER
⅛ TEASPOON SALT
DASH OF PEPPER
1 TABLESPOON BUTTER

1. In a bowl combine eggs, water, salt, and dash of pepper.
2. Using a fork, beat until combined but not frothy.

3. In an 8- or 10-inch skillet with flared sides, heat butter, lifting and tilting the pan to coat the sides.

4. Add egg mixture to skillet. Cook over medium heat. As eggs set, run a spatula around the edge and let the uncooked eggs flow underneath.

5. Add fillings. Fold the omelet in half and serve immediately.

TABLE FOR TWENTY

Preparing a gathering for 20 can be as easy as preparing one for 10 if you plan, delegate, and know the proper amounts to prepare or to ask your guests to bring.

SOUP AND SALAD SUPPER MENU

- Salads—4 heads of lettuce; separate other salad items into 1 to 2 cup servings to be tossed prior to the meal.
- Dressings—1 pint per flavor, if serving at least three flavors
- Crackers—1½ pounds
- Soups—1 gallon per flavor, if you are serving at least three flavors
- Cheese—1½ pounds (3 pounds if everyone will be offered a 2-ounce serving)
- Coffee—½ pound and 1½ gallons water
- Tea—½ pound and 1½ gallons water

BUFFET PRESENTATION AND SERVING

The best way to feed a large group is to let them bring their own and serve themselves. However, we have all been in line behind the overfillers. If this is a persistent problem among the flock, make a humorous announcement prior to the partaking. Say something like, "Everyone has arrived at the dinner in hopes of eating a plateful, so please make sure your cup is not running over."

Achieving ambience is an exercise in creative, low-budget thinking. Position the foods in order of usual eating preference. You may want to create heights to the buffet table by stacking books or placing boxes on the tables prior to putting on the tablecloths. This would make space available for twisting and turning English ivy from Deacon Jones' backyard into a lovely presentation for the buffet table. That same theme could be carried out on the individual tables. Tie colorful ribbons leftover from Sister Susie's wedding arrangements and call it decorated.

DECORATING

Here are some suggestions for quick and easy centerpieces:

- Set votive candles in small canning jars.
- Roll down small, brown paper lunch sacks and set a small flowering plant inside each.
- Place baskets full of seasonal fruit in the center of the table.
- Prior to the dinner, have the children's Sunday school classes draw their favorite part of church, and place the drawings down the center of the tables.
- Collect single bud vases from different church members and label

them so returning will be simplified. Place the vases down the center of the tables, and stick a different colored Gerber daisy in each vase.

- Ask each family to bring a new stuffed animal, and set the animals down the center of the tables. Donate these toys to a children's home or homeless shelter. (Use this idea in May or June when the under-privileged children would least expect a gift.)
- Place doilies down the center of the tables and have the youth group bake and decorate large cupcakes and top with a stemmed cherry. Set the cupcakes on the doilies. This is a pretty, eatable table decoration.
- Place clean terra cotta pots down the center of the tables and fill them with skinny loaves of French bread.
- Fill extra water pitchers with water and fresh daisies. Place one on each table.
- Splatter-paint old, small vegetable crates, turn them upside down on each table, and place the water and tea pitchers on top.

GREETERS

Someone on the covered dish planning committee should be assigned the greeting and hospitality duties. The size of your dinner crowd determines how many people are needed to act as hosts and hostesses to herd the throngs along through the buffet and on to their tables. A food monitor makes sure the buffet keeps running smoothly and that empty dishes are removed and replaced with other dishes. The monitor makes sure second-timers are not ahead of the others. These folks should also make welcome any new members and visitors.

SEATING

Seating is essential to a smooth social. One suggestion is to seat everyone first, offer thanks, and queue up the buffet line by tables (first table from the door goes first). This will keep your waiting-in-line time shorter.

DINNER ON
THE GROUNDS

When the social is combined with a cemetery cleaning or the church wants to dine on the new building property, your food needs become a different story. Planning, preparation, and much perseverance are necessary to pull off this party. One must expect to endure many little inconveniences—a small bug or pesky flies—but effort should be taken in keeping the sandwiches from tasting like bananas and the corn salad like cake.

This section contains suggestions for dinner on the grounds, a folding chair phenomenon that is the backbone of down-home good eatin', a solid rock of the religion of fine food.

BASIC SETUP

1. Table and chair delivery and setup are the first steps to readying the grounds. The committee needs an estimated count of attendees so as to have proper tables and seating. Set up under a shady area if possible, or rent a reduced-sized revival tent. (This could assure that the fellowship would continue if weather was a problem.) Make sure sprinkler systems will not activate during your event.

2. Cover the tables with butcher paper, and tape the ends and sides underneath the table. This serves two purposes: one, it keeps the good cloths preserved and, two, the children's tables can have crayons provided for entertainment during and after the dinner.

3. The buffet tables should be set in an area where two lines can be formed, preferably out of direct sunlight so as not to overheat the potato salad. Set a separate area with tables for the desserts, ice and drinks, and disposals.

4. Sturdy paper products are a must. Paper plates work best if they are divided into segments to keep foods from running together. Somehow the segments are never quite big enough to accommodate the giant servings that covered dish regulars seem to require when food is served in the open air, so bring extra plates.

5. Enlist young people to wrap plastic eating utensils with large dinner-size paper napkins and tie with a ribbon. Place the utensils in a large basket at the end of the buffet line so that two hands can be used while filling up the plate.

BASIC SUPPLIES FOR THE REMOTE COVERED DISH

EATING UTENSILS

- plates
- plastic glasses
- Styrofoam cups
- flatware
- napkins
- serving utensils
- tablecloth
- groundcloth
- placemats
- plastic tablecloth to cover picnic foods in case of a sudden rainstorm

STAPLES

- closable salt and pepper shakers, or regular shaker tops covered with masking tape to limit spills
- sugar packets in an airtight container
- water jug
- small carving board

CLEANUP

- plastic garbage bags
- wet wipes
- paper towels
- duct tape
- sponges and washcloths
- aluminum foil

CARRYING THE MEAL

If you need to travel with your dish, here are some suggestions for having everything you might need to make your outing comfortable and easy.

1. You do not have to have the most fashionable picnic basket in order to take your covered dish on the road. The "basic basket" need not be a basket at all. The least expensive alternative is a cardboard file storage box. Line the inside with an adhesive-backed vinyl for easy cleanup.

2. Line a pretty basket with a brightly colored dish cloth, and place your covered dish inside. This method is best for dishes that do not require insulation.

3. For foods that require cooling, purchase pieces of polyurethane foam, available in fabric stores. This makes a great insulator when glued into wicker baskets. Cut 1-inch-thick pieces of foam to line the top, bottom, and sides of the basket. Add thoroughly chilled items and cover the basket tightly. Place the basket in a shaded area, and foods will stay cold for up to 4 hours.

4. To keep a tossed salad cool, select a large bushel basket (available at many farmers' markets) and place your greens in a large, covered container that will fit loosely into your basket. Line the basket with a heavy garbage bag, place a layer of cracked ice in the bag, insert the salad container, and fill in with extra ice. A salad dressing, in a separate, tightly covered jar, can be put in the basket too.

5. Round baskets layered with newspaper will help keep hot foods hot. Wrap the hot dish in heavy foil, and place it on the newspapers. Cover with another layer of newspapers, and top with a towel.

6. Consider these other ideas for keeping foods at their proper temperatures:
   - Coolers
   - Ice substitutes—gels available in plastic containers; freeze prior to event
   - Refrigerator bags—vinyl, insulated bags that close with a zipper
   - Thermal containers—be sure to heat or chill container before adding food or drink

FIRST AID

Being prepared whatever the circumstance is a necessary motto when dealing with large groups. Make sure a first-aid kit is packed with your other essentials.

Be sure to include these items:
- first-aid booklet
- thermometer
- ice bags
- adhesive tape
- gauze
- self-stick bandages
- alcohol pads
- antibacterial soap and washcloth
- tweezers
- aspirin
- antacid tablets
- calamine lotion
- insect spray
- sunscreen

FAMILY
REUNIONS

F amily reunions combine generations filled with riotous reminiscing and hopeful visions of the future. We can remember crusty, cheese-topped macaroni, shoe peg corn fried in real butter, and fresh coconut cake that appeared to be as high as the sky. The family gathering helps to link all generations, both past and present. While everyone asks each other questions such as "How are you?" or "How old are you now?" the real question on their minds is "When are we going to eat?"

We remember showing up at the family reunion and looking forward to seeing our cool cousins from the other side of the United States. As kids, the thought of planning never entered our minds. However, those long tables overflowing with delectable delights that were served under the huge trees did not just appear out of the blue. Plenty of planning went into these parties. The following information will give you an easy-to-follow game plan for your next big reunion.

MAKING PREPARATIONS

1. *Select the date:* At least 6 months in advance gives everyone a good lead time for planning their family's schedule. Summer months are best.

2. *Form a planning committee:* Especially if your family is large, you might want to ask people from the different branches of the family to gather current addresses, build enthusiasm, and dispense and receive information during the planning months.

3. *Select a location:* Is there a tried-and-true gathering place? A family farm, backyard, or lake? Keep in mind the needs for water, restrooms, and electricity for entertaining, cooking, and lights. What is plan B in case of bad weather?

4. *Send communication and invitations:* Information should include: who, what, when, where (with a map), and how much (if expenses are to be shared). Send a form requesting biographical information on each person, including age, interests, and achievements. A newsletter builds enthusiasm and encourages attendance.

5. *Determine the menu and related needs:* This can be potluck, catered, assigned, or a combination. For a large gathering, appoint a treasurer. A committee for tables, chairs, ice, water, paper goods, and garbage disposal is a good idea.

6. *Choose a master of ceremonies:* Select someone to give direction and guide the day's activities through the planned events.

7. *Pick out a photographer:* Appoint an official photographer and encourage everyone to share individual pictures with others afterwards.

SCHEDULING A DAY'S EVENTS

1. Remember the needs of people of all ages. Plan relaxing times for older participants and the very young.

2. Provide activities for teens to break the ice with tapes, games, and snacks.

3. Include as many people as possible in the entertainment. Teens may enjoy organizing younger children and teaching them songs and routines. Children too shy to speak may sing in a group.

4. Storytelling is the heart of a great reunion. Request favorite stories from everyone whether they attend or not, and have a storytelling time.

5. Use information received from biographical sheets to organize a talent show.

6. Build a family tree of snapshots brought to the reunion. Request these early from everyone whether they attend or not.

7. Print a schedule of events so everyone shows up on time. Designate a relaxed time for leisurely visits and rest.

8. Remember necessary equipment for home videos and movies.

9. Try a family memorabilia table. Lots of surprises show up here.

10. Keep an official registration book for everyone to sign, and bring it to future reunions.

11. Before the reunion draws to a close, propose a time for the next gathering. Someone present may offer to host the next one.

12. For those unable to attend, as well as those present, compile addresses, biographical information, and highlights of the time together as a memento.

BLESSINGS

1. Now before we eat today,
   We will not forget to pray
   To God, who kept us through the night
   And brought us to the morning light.
   —Charles Cabaniss

2. We thank you for our food, dear Lord.
   We lift our voice in one accord.
   You bring us food from hands unknown.
   The glory of your countenance shown.
   It strengthens us throughout the day.
   In Jesus' holy name we pray.
   —Charles Cabaniss

3. Thanks be unto God
    Whose kindness gives
    This food on which our bodies live. Amen.
    —Charles Cabaniss

4. Lord, make us thankful for our blessings.
    Bless this food to our bodies,
    Forgive us our sins,
    And save us at last in Thy kingdom.
    For Christ's sake. Amen
    —Traditional

5. Father accept our thanks
    For these and all our blessings. Amen.
    —Traditional

6. For food and all Thy gifts of love,
    We give Thee thanks and praise.
    Look down, O Father, from above,
    And bless us all our days. Amen.
    —Traditional

7. God is Great
    God is Good
    And we thank him for this food.
    By his hand we all are fed
    Give us O Lord our daily bread.
    —Traditional

8. Be present at our Table Lord
   Be here and everywhere adored
   These creatures bless and grant that we
   May feast in Paradise with thee.
   We thank thee Lord for this our food
   But more because of Jesus' love
   Let manna to our Souls be given
   The bread of Life sent down from Heaven.
   —John Cennick, 1741, as inscribed on the
      Wesley-Wedgewood teapot

RECIPES FOR
LIFE

A RECIPE ONE SHOULD KNOW AND REMEMBER

For God so loved the world, that he gave his only begotten Son, that whosoever believeth in him should not perish, but have everlasting life (John 3:16).

There are several things you should know about this Recipe.

1. *You need to follow its instructions.* "For all have sinned, and come short of the glory of God," (Rom. 3:23). "There is none righteous, no, not one" (Rom. 3:10). (See also Jer. 17:9; Isa. 64:6; Isa. 53:6; John 3:3).

2. *You can't change any of its ingredients; in other words, you can't save yourself.* "There is a way which seemeth right unto a man, but the end thereof are the ways of death" (Prov. 14:12). Jesus Christ is the only One that can save us (Acts 4:12). (See also Gal. 2:16; Jas. 2:10; Titus 3:5).

3. *Salvation has been provided for you through Jesus Christ.* "Christ Jesus came into the world to save sinners" (1 Tim. 1:15). "Who his own self bare our sins in his own body on the tree" (1 Peter 2:24). (See also Heb. 2:9; John 3:16).

4. *You will receive the results of this Recipe if you will place your trust in Christ.* "Believe on the Lord Jesus Christ, and thou shalt be saved" (Acts 16:31). When you do this, you show repentance toward God and faith toward our Lord Jesus Christ. You also confess your sins to God.

We hope that soon you can say: "Knowing that I am a sinner and knowing that Jesus Christ died for me, I now accept Him as my Savior, and with His help I will witness concerning Him before men" for "with the mouth confession is made unto salvation" (Rom. 10:10).

RECIPE FOR A CHRISTIAN HOME

Combine together in needed quantities:

Family worship

Individual meditation

Purposeful prayer

Regular church attendance

Love for one another

Add all at one time to:

Christian parents—any number
of children

Flavor with one each of:

Happy disposition

Dash of thoughtfulness

Hint of tact

Manners to taste, and

Unmeasured kindness

Omit:

Tempers

Nagging

Jealousy

For best results, include plenty of patience. Mixture will keep indefinitely and serve an entire community generously.

FOR TODAY

2 cups Love	1 cup Friendliness
1 cup Kindness	4 teaspoons Gentleness
1 pound Joy	1 large box Faith
1 pound Peace	1 pound Long-suffering
1 box Meekness	1 pinch Humor

Mix all together with concern. Bake in an oven of forgiveness one hour, with Prayer. Cool on the table of understanding and serve with compassion.

PRESERVING CHILDREN

1 large grassy field	Narrow strip of brook
6 children, all sizes	(pebbly if possible)
3 small dogs (rat terriers preferred)	Hot sun
Deep, blue skies	Flowers

Mix the children with the dogs and empty into the field, stirring continuously. Sprinkle the field with flowers, pour brook gently over the pebbles. Cover all with deep, blue skies and bake in hot sun. When children are well browned, they may be removed, and they will be found right and ready for setting away to cool in the bathtub.

RECIPE FOR FRIENDSHIP

Take two heaping cups of patience
One heart full of love
Two hands full of generosity
A dash of laughter
One head full of understanding
Sprinkle generously with kindness
Add plenty of faith and mix well
Spread over a period of a lifetime and
Serve everybody you meet.

HOW TO COOK A HUSBAND

A good many husbands are entirely spoiled by mismanagement in cooking and so are not tender and good. Some women go about it as if their husbands were bladders and blow them up. Others keep them constantly in hot water, while others let them freeze by their carelessness and indifference. Some keep them in a stew by irritating ways and words. Others roast them, and some keep them in a pickle all their lives.

It cannot be supposed that any husband will be tender and good, managed in this way; but they really are delicious when properly treated. In selecting your husband, you should not be guided by the silvery appearance, as in buying mackerel, nor by the golden tint, as if you wanted salmon. Be sure and select him yourself, as tastes differ. Do not go to market for him, as the best is always brought to the door. It is far better to have none, unless you will patiently learn how to cook him.

A preserving kettle of the finest porcelain is the best, but if you have nothing but an earthenware pipkin, it will do with care. See that the linen in which you wrap him is nicely washed and mended with the requisite number of buttons and strings nicely sewed on. Tie him in the kettle by a strong silken cord called comfort; duty is apt to be weak. Husbands are apt to fly out of the kettle and be burned and crusty on the edge, since like crabs and lobsters you have to cook them while alive. Make a clear, steady fire out of love, neatness, and cheerfulness. Set your husband as near to this as seems to agree with him. If he sputters and fizzes, do not be anxious; some husbands do this until they are quite done. Add a little sugaring, the form of what confectioners call kisses, but not vinegar or pepper on any account. A little spice improves him, but it must be used with judgment. Do not stick any sharp instrument into him to see if he is becoming tender. Stir him gently; watch the smile, lest he lie too flat and close to the kettle so as to become useless. You cannot fail to know when he is done. If thus treated you will find him very digestible, agreeing nicely with you and the children, and he will keep as long as you want unless you become careless and set him in too cold a place.

INDEX OF
RECIPES

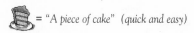 = *"A piece of cake"* *(quick and easy)*

APPETIZERS

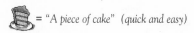

SALADS AND SOUPS

BREADS

MAIN DISHES